Can I Have Your Charm Bracelet When You Die?

A DUBLIN CHILDHOOD

By Sheila Hamilton

hens teeth publishing

CAN I HAVE YOUR CHARM BRACELET WHEN YOU DIE?

First published in 2024 by
Hens Teeth Publishing
Irishtown
Dublin 4
Ireland

Print ISBN: 978-1-0687505-0-2
eBook ISBN: 978-1-0687505-1-9

Editorial Assistance: Luke Hamilton & Séamus Ó Maithiú

Cover Photography by Wayne Fitzgerald

Graphic Design: Artwerk Limited

www.hensteethpublishing.com

Dedication

This book is dedicated to my wonderful mother,
Elizabeth McQuillan Hamilton,
and to my gorgeous
auntie Esther & Nanny,
thank you for loving me.

Some Honourable Mentions

To my love, for being with me every step of the way.

To my family and dearest friends.

To the friends that are no longer here, but always with us.

To the ones who make us laugh, you know who you are!

To Ireland, for the madness, the culture, the characters.

But most especially, to Dubliners,

Thank you.

This story is based on actual events. Some details, regarding, my childhood, life, family, timelines and people involved have been changed. Some characters are a combination of two or more people. In certain cases, timelines and characters may be sprinkled with the lightest embellishment of a fuzzy memory, or a fanciful childhood imagination, and all are shared with love.

Nanny's House

The navy-blue night sky crackles with worry and excitement. Not a sinner on the road but for the odd rattling of a car that might ramble by. My auntie Esther and me standing in the window waiting for my grandmother to come home on the bus.

'She should have been home by now, it's getting very late ... Sure, she's probably talking to someone, you know what your Nanny's like', Esther says, consoling herself with a forced smile. Nanny went to the Bingo at the National Stadium almost every night.

'But the 22a should have been here by now', Esther's voice fatal, the net curtains pulled right back to get a clear view. Me, hanging onto every word, eyes peering out while my breath hits the glass, the terror of losing my Nanny to the empty night makes my heart thump. This ritual continues most nights whether the bus is late, or not. Esther is the nervous type.

Some days she cries ...

This morning, I wake up late to Tammy Wynette singing on the stereo; *Our D.I.V.O.R.C.E. becomes final today.* Nanny and Esther are already up cooking my breakfast, lighting the fire, and putting the dinner on. I came to stay with them when I was a baby, I'm told.

My earliest memories are of standing in the yellow basin on the table in my grandmother's kitchen. Warm water soothes my three-year-old back.

1

The smell of Dettol, Polytar shampoo, boiled ribs, and cabbage wafts around my suddy head. Her hands are coarse and red from cleaning.

'Close your eyes tight.' Her fine-boned nose touches mine; her sparkling blue eyes dance bright as she scoops me in a towel. Her beautiful face, interrupted by falling auburn curls.

Esther is my aunt, my minder, defender, slave and best friend. I am barely six years old; she is twenty-something and lives in my father's mother's house, a two up-two down, in working-class Dublin, with my grandmother, grandfather, and me. This home, a delightful mix of worn furniture, smoky fire, small and large bodies, shouting, talking, laughing, is the centre of all my universe.

Pig's feet, ribs, coddle or stew; on the boil, day or night, to feed some of her thirteen children or their children, all of whom visit regularly. Meat so fatty and soft that it falls off the bone as steam fills the air with a salty, greasy deliciousness. Roast beef on Sundays, set in a large pot of pure animal fat, 'drippin.' This left-over fat, with the flavour and juices from the meat cooks the food for the rest of the week. Fried bread, my favourite, 'Sit down and ate that', served with two runny fried eggs, sausage and pudding. I have never since smelled or tasted anything like it.

Nanny's house is made all the more exciting by morning deliveries of fresh bread and cakes from Barney, the breadman. Usually, an uncut crusty square of bread called 'turnover', my Nanny pronounces 'turrinn-over' is delivered, and enjoyed with what can only be described as a doorstep of butter.

When the horn beeps, I run past my Nanny through the front garden and little red gate to the back of his truck. Dancing with excitement, eyes popping, mouthwatering as trays of pink square ice cakes, lemon drizzle, tipsy cakes, and apple cream pies, are slid out on wooden boards into the light.

'Come back, I've to give you the money. Come back, I said,' she shouts after me.

Decorated with solid gold sovereigns and large coloured stones, her old ringed fingers root in her smock pocket to produce a worn pound note; 'Ask Barney for six snow cakes, and a turrinn-over. I haven't the money for anything else, so don't ask him!'

'Can I have six snow cakes, a 'turrinn-over' and an apple cream pie please Barney?', I say, then take a big bite out of the apple cream pie so I don't have to give it back. I then run and tell her she hasn't enough money.

'What did I tell you to do?', she says, exasperated; 'I told you I hadn't the money for anything else. You're leaving me without a shillin, you're very bold!'

'Sorry Nanny', (and not a bit sorry), I skip down the garden, frilly dress, red pigtails swinging. She shouts out to no one in particular, 'That young one's very impertnint!'

Every morning at nine, all mats are lined up outside and beaten within an inch of their lives, then shortly after, scrubbed along with the floors, doors, steps, and me. This morning is no different. Esther is scrubbing the rug on the steps in the sun as Nanny tiptoes out the door; Lilly is never in, well, not until dinner time anyway.

Kind, smiling and round, Nanny proudly wears a pink and white gingham 'smock' over her clothes like a badge of honour, every day, except Sundays. Pockets sufficiently deep to hold rolls of notes on a good day of selling, and fistfuls of coins on any other. She sells 'Fruit and veg, of a Monday, Wednesday and Saturday, fish of a Tuesday and Friday.' Every Saturday, her grey hair is set in rollers at the hairdressers; this produces coil tight 'curdilles' (curls) that frame her ears that hold her thick, gold, spikey hoop earrings.

Shining in the sun, outside her almost always open front door, stands her pride and joy, her work, her freedom, her livelihood, her independence. A big old Silver Cross pram. Years since it carried her babies, it now transports her stock to and from the market. She walks 'five mile' to the market, down Cloghar Road, onto Leonards Corner, down Clanbrassil Street, through to Patrick's Street, up the hill to Christchurch, down the hill at Christchurch, past the Four Courts and into Smithfield. Then, loaded with her cargo, she walks back up the steep hill towards home, selling her stock to the many guesthouses, B&Bs and businesses, along the way. Little do I know as I hold her hand, I too will walk these same streets one day.

Her customers, mostly Jewish, had come to Dublin before and after the Holocaust. They set up their businesses in 'Little Jerusalem'. I love walking by the synagogue.

Lyrical and soothing, raised voices in prayer, the strange eastern European accents. The respect and reverence shown to my grandmother. 'Oh, Lilly, wait till I tell you, come in come in' - the hushed gossip and dramatic hand gestures in the kosher butchers, owned by her good friend, Baila Erlich.

'That's shockin Baila, may God forgive them', my grandmother, a devout Catholic, rated kindness above any religion, and when she met the Rabbi, they held hands and greeted each other as friends.

She also has a penchant for 'the slots' ... the one-armed bandits. Sometimes, on the way back from town or a day's work, she slips in to play them, 'Don't tell anyone, do you hear me? Don't say a word to Esther or any of them, about me playing the slots.'

'No, Nanny I won't!', I promise. Only the minute I get through the door; 'Me Nanny was in the slots!', I hang her out to dry.

'I hope you didn't lose your day's money in the slots, Mammy?', Esther scolds.

'I thought you weren't going in there anymore. The last time you said the machine jammed as you were about to win!' Esther winks, and my aunts laugh.

'Go long outa dat and mind yis are own business!', my Nanny tells them as she darts me a look.

Esther dresses me in white, lavender, pink and lemon, frilly dresses, petticoats, ribbons, and bows. She even got my ears pierced last year when I was five years old after I threw myself in a puddle screaming and crying because my cousin had gotten hers done first. 'She's after makin a holy show of me in town', she tells my aunts, stifling giggles and showing off my new emerald gold earrings.

Most Saturdays, we go to Meath Street to go shopping with my aunts. This means chip sandwiches with salt and vinegar, on freshly baked bread with melting butter, cream cakes, pots of tea, buying, gossiping and me earwigging. And almost every Sunday morning, my grandfather brings me to the local sports club, his trilby hat at a jaunty angle, his tired, thin frame, clean worn suit, holding my hand as we stroll up the road for his Sunday morning pint, my crisps, and glass of red lemonade.

I enjoy the drama-filled days the best; 'Quick, here's the insurance man; get under the stairs!', Esther screams in a whisper. Me, Nanny and Esther sitting in the dark under the stairs, door shut until he got tired of knocking and went away. There was no money to pay him.

Tonight, the 22a double-decker bus appears like a star to a wise man, chucks up the road and drops off the precious cargo. There, standing on the path, a bag over one arm and lopsided by the weight of another, her powder blue coat stretched and buttoned in the middle, like a belt around a pillow, is my Nanny, big, soft and beautiful.

'It's very late Mammy, where were you?', probes Esther.

'I was talking to poor Mr Kavanagh; he's broken-hearted over poor Mrs Kavanagh, the poor man. I told him to pray to the Blessed Virgin for comfort. Pass me me slippers.' Nanny throws herself down as she kicks off her sandals, her feet swollen with bunions, her knees bandaged from pushing her pram. 'I won the carriage clock', she tells me triumphantly. The carriage clock: a beautiful decorative display of gold lamé and intricate plastic moulding, adorns her mantelpiece for years to come.

Some days, when I feel like it, she brings me to the stations of the cross or mass. I watch her as she mumbles her prayers, blesses herself, lights candles (I insist on helping) and rolls her rosary beads through her fingers

6

in a deep trance-like state. Her devotion and sincere belief in the power of prayer are her solace and strength throughout her life. When she's finished, we waddle home, humming and eating toffees. I am blessed. It is my world. They belong to me.

They love me unconditionally.

Esther

'Isn't Bobby Ewing only gorgeous', she tells me more than asks. The American hard gum wedged in the side of her mouth as she speaks, 'Ah jaysus he's gorgeous' she's now leaning out of her armchair at the side of the fire.

'Move back Esther' I tell her, 'If you fall in, you'll be burned alive.' I'm only six years old, and even I know that. She ignores me, leans forward, elbows on her knees, unconsciously eating her sweets, and without even offering me one. Though I already had a quarter of my own, I was fed up with my pink Bon Bons and was in need of a change; 'Can I have one of yours please?' She passes me the brown paper bag without looking. *Dallas* is on the television, and she doesn't want to talk to me. I have to be quiet at this time every Thursday night.

Granda works on the docks, shift work, and if he's not in bed, he's out with his pals.

Nanny is in the corner eating her toffees, there's no bingo on tonight. In between unwrapping and stuffing her mouth with buttery toffee cubes, she takes small rectangular pieces of paper from her bag, and, one at a time, looks at the picture, mumbles to herself and puts it back into the bag. The bag looks like the chewed toffee in her mouth, brown, shiny, and squashed.

'What are you doing Nanny?', I interrupt.

'Sayin me prayers, shush', she tries to shut me up.

'Are you not watching *Dallas* with us Nanny' I insist.

'Shushsh, in a minute' she quips.

'Will I help you Nanny?', I offer her.

'No!', her unappreciative response shrugs my shoulders.

'Shushsh', Esther waves her left arm in the air 'Watch, here's *Sue Ellen*. Oh God love her. Is she drunk? Oh here's *J.R.* Aw no. Aw leave her alone! Aw he's shouting at her! Ahh she's in an awful state. Ohhh! Don't! Ah leave her alone! Ah don't. Oh Mammy! Look, look! Awwwhh! He's sneerin at her. Awwwwhh! Look what he's after doing to her. Ah God help her. Ah look at her crying!', Esther gasps.

'Why did he do that? Why did he do it Esther?', I ask, confused, and only half interested.

She ignores me again; 'He's taking the child off her! Ah, look at her crying. He's taking the child. She's breaking her heart crying.' Esther sniffs and pats her eyes with a tissue. This was only *Dallas*, *Imitation of Life* caused a torrential flood of tears, her eyes swollen for days. I didn't understand or like it very much, as everyone was crying inside the television, and out.

'WAIT! Oh! Oh! Look! SHE'S grabbing him. She's slapping him, good girdle yourself! Give it to him! Give it to him!', she roars at the television.

'DAT FELLAS ONLY A BASTARD!', Nanny erupts from her corner on the couch. The room is silent for a full three seconds.

'Nanny!', I exclaim.

'Mammy!', Esther sits back open-mouthed. We are both incredulous, surprised, and shocked by my Nanny's explosion of profanity.

'She never curses!', I tell Esther. We both stare at my Nanny, demanding an explanation. She gives us none. But as gravely as I have ever seen her, she moves her head from side to side, stunned by her outburst, and slowly blesses herself; 'May God forgive me for using that foul language. May God forgive me.'

Esther rocks with laughter. Covering her mouth with her hand she tries to contain her hysterics. She can't, and eventually lets out a searing shriek. She is soon rolling off her chair in convulsions of laughter, as too am I. By now, Nanny's body is chuckling in the corner, her big smile, gentle grey curls, childlike face and glistening grey-blue eyes streaming with tears of amusement brought on by her own blasphemous outburst. There we were, *J.R., Sue Ellen,* and our happy little trio, rolling around the front room of 509 on a chilly summer's evening.

The following Saturday, a glorious sunny morning, Esther was up at the crack of dawn. She was going out tonight and was taking no prisoners; 'Stay on that couch and don't move. Here's your breakfast.' The house was tussled, tackled, terrorized, and tamed by 10am. Meath Street shopping attacked and conquered by noon. The stew lacerated and lashed on by two.

Clothes twin tubbed, flung and hung by four. Her suit pressed and her body showered by 5pm. The 'do' was in the local workman's club, Dickie Rock was playing and 'spit on me Dickie' didn't wait for anyone.

'You have to be early to get a good table, that's why I want to be ready by seven' she tells me on her hands and knees scrubbing the front steps.

'Will you get me the make-up bag and hot rollers

10

under the stairs', she points to the coalhouse. Like everything else it is immaculately clean and lined with fresh newspaper every other day.

Her thick, auburn red hair had been washed and blow-dried. Lined up on the table are her brushes, combs, pins, and hairspray.

'You pass me the pins when I've a roller in me hair,' this was a serious business, and I was ready.

She separates her hair with a tail comb, rolls the hot roller tightly and commands a pin from me. Before long, her head is full of large, spikey sausages. They are then sprayed with the rotten-smelling hairspray; 'Mind your eyes.' That done, she is on to her tan.

'Always dampen the sponge before you put your tan on', she instructs; 'If you don't, it won't be even, and you'll be like Farreller Dempsey's piebald pony.'

'Now pass me the make-up bag please', she says as she squeezes the large yellow sponge over a warm basin of water.

'I'll do it', I say, opening her bag.

'No not today. Here, there's one for you, stick the brush in it' she says as she hands me a used lipstick.

'See that pan stick?', she opens a gold and navy tube; 'Don't put that on until you moisturise your face first, or you'll be like your aunty Margret, with a face like a patchwork quilt', she giggles, so do I. Margret, my uncle Willie's wife, was unbeknownst to her, the butt of many jokes. And according to Esther, the proprietor of 'Corned beef legs, straight hair and wavy teeth.'

'Don't say I said that there'll be murder!', she whispers.

'SHUSH! What's that? Who's that coming in the gate?

Quick hide, it's your uncle Willie he's drunk!', she belts past me into the kitchen. Tugging my cardigan attached to my back.

'Get in, stay down, shush!', her eyes peeking over the countertop. The front door knocker bangs off the hinges, and we hear him talking to himself.

'Es me muthur dur pleeesehuuh, plehuuh, plehuuheeese. I know you're in der, I'm only comin to say hellouuh!', he says, hiccupping through the letterbox.

'Why won't you let him in?', I whisper to her on my hunkers as I fiddle with the frill on my newly acquired ankle socks. Her voice barely audible, she replies, her finger over her mouth, 'Cos he's looking for money for drink and he'll have me scourged if I let him in.'

BANG, BANG, BANG

'Open the door, Esther. Have u got a loan of a fiver, huh, please? Margret locked me out, and I want to keep drinking!', he hollers through the hall door.

After cursing him under her breath she springs to her feet.

'I'M NOT IN!', she shouts at the top of her lungs, her patience spent; 'STOP bangin the door; Mary next door is lying down, she's not well!'

'Ah der ye are, let us in pleuusehuh!', he shouts back through the letterbox. She marches to the door and swipes it open. There he is, leaning against the wall like an s hook. A smiling, handsome folded heap.

'What do you want, you're not comin in here full a drink', her sharp words reflected in his face; his warm toothy smile fades into his hurt furrowed brows.

His muscular, tanned arm wipes the sweat from his

dripping hair. He straightens up like a dishevelled child. His innocence, both charming and disarming as he pulls at his too-tight T-shirt.

'I only called to see how you were if you needhuh anything', he tells her most sincerely.

He's about to step into the hall.

'Get off me floors. Stay there, ye can't come in. Stay on that newspaper I'm only after washing them floors!', she tells him.

'Sssorry, where's me muther?', he asks.

'She's gone out!', she snaps.

'Ou, she's never in!', he says.

Then he sees me and offers me his large, rough palm; 'Aw Shelly I didn't know you were here. Here an I give you a few bob', he searches deep into his pockets and hands me a sprinkle of dark halfpenny coins, mixed with fluff and crumbs. His kindness, never eclipsed by his drinking, he rubs my hand, 'Esther minding you?'

I smile back. I think back to the time just the previous summer when he brought me to Meath Street and carried me all the way home on his shoulders in the burning sun, having spent his bus fare buying me an ice-cream. 'She was lying on the ground screaming for a Cornetto, I didn't know what to do!', he told Esther. She interrupts our exchange; 'No, I don't need anything. I'm grand thanks', she tells him as she motions at shutting the door.

'You need to go home!'

He slides down the wall, landing on the step, 'I'm not goin home uuuhh, have you a loan of a fiver plseeease? Your hair's lovely', he tells her as he slouches his elbows tucked under his arms, his roasted dripping, amber face tilted to the sun.

'I'm sure it is! Where are you going?', she looks at her watch.

'I'm only going to the Countess for one drink, then I'm getting fish n chips and going straight huupp home. I wouldn't huuh lie to you' he tells her, his eyes large and glazed, his eyebrows raised and vigilant to see if she's buying his story.

A sarcastic smile appears on her lips; 'You wouldn't whaa? You wouldn't lie to me? Sure, you're a confounded liar, you can't tell the truth! I thought you were coming on Thursday to do me yard. Did I see you? No! Last Saturday you said you were coming 'without fail' to clean me windows? Did you show up? No! And you're telling me now, you wouldn't lie to me? Looking for a fiver off me? Well, you're not getting a shillin off me! I'm not giving it to you!', she tells him as she puts her hand on the door to close it.

With that, he leaps up, puts his hand on the door and begs her, 'Please, ah please, I promise you on me mother's life I'll be up to you tomorrow to do it for you, please!' She's trying not to laugh and as she pretends to be shutting the door, she shouts; 'Tomorrow! Tomorrow you won't know your own religion tomorrow and don't be swearin on me mother's life, swear on your own, or Margret's!'

'I meant Monday', he quickly interrupts, 'I meant I'll do it for you Monday! Ah stop, stop, I promise you, have I ever let you down before, have I? I always do the garden and windows for you, go on please, give us the fiver?', his pleading finally working when she walks inside to get him

14

the money. She shoves the scrunched five-pound note into his hand 'Go on and then go straight home, do you hear me!' His wide grin returns; he tosses his hair, puts his fists in the air and jumps in front of her like a prize fighter.

'Put em up, put em up!', he tells her.'

She pushes his fists away laughing, 'Go on! You would! It would be the first and last time, you effin eejit! Go on home.'

He walks off laughing and singing but remarkably steady, bolstered by his newfound fortune.

'Thanks, you're very good, I'll see you Monday', he calls back and whistles into the distance. She watches him smiling. Despite her weekly protestations that she's 'Finished with him' and that 'He'll never as long as he lives get another shillin off me!', she would always relent; he was, after all, her brother.

'Look what time it is, come on, I'll be dead late!', she slams the door.

In front of the large, gold framed mirror that hangs over the varnished wood mantel piece she carefully adorns her delicate features. Olive green shadow, black soot mascara, peach blush, and palest pink lipstick, are stroked, pushed and patted onto her translucent skin.

Without saying a word, she bounces onto the armchair, turns on her stereo, drops the needle and blasts Dolly Parton's *Jolene.*

With arms outstretched, she hops down, kicks off her slip-on's, grabs my hands and swings me around the room. Together we sing, our voices as loud as the record player, both on full volume. As the song ends, we collapse breathless and laughing onto the couch. My joy disappears with the fading music as it dawns on me, she will soon be going out. The sky turns dark as the angry rain lashes the window we can no longer see through. A morbid gloom burgles the room and my heart.

'Will Nanny mind me tonight?', I ask.

'Yes', she replies, her hand on her chest and smiling; 'I'm barely able to breathe. Sarah's gonna stay and you're gonna have a party.' Not even Sarah, who is my very favourite cousin, can console my troubled heart.

'I don't want you to go' I whimper.

'Why? Do you think I wouldn't come back? I'd leave you?', she smiles, dropping her dainty brow to touch mine. I nod my head up and down.

'Leave you? Leave you! The apple of me eye! Are you mad?', she hugs me, 'I wouldn't leave you in a million years! Not in a million years! I'll be home early; I promise you and you can stay in the bed with me.' Instantly I feel better, reassured by her words, comforted by her cuddles.

Forty minutes later, she appears in the middle of the room like a pleased peacock.

Her auburn red coiffed curls catching the yellow rays as the sun brazens its way back into the evening summer sky. A cream jacket and knee-length skirt draped over a pale pink silk camisole, worn with a solid gold chain. With her nude high heels and beautifully bronzed legs, she is a perched and stunning vision to behold, all five foot two inches of her.

But her gold charm bracelet dangling from her dainty wrist is her pièce de résistance. Mesmerised, captivated and hypnotised by the magical, glistening gemstones, the sparkling, intricate charms, the horseshoe links and the gold heart lock, I beg her to try it on.

'Not now, tomorrow I promise you ... It was only a shower, anyway, thank God.' she says. 'Do you think I'll see me fella tonight? Marina Byrne said he'd a new girlfriend, but I don't believe it, sure he told me he loved me, how could he forget about me?', she asks me as she dips her head, widens her eyes, and poses with a smile. A wayward teapot lid clatters in the background; Nanny has returned and is making the tea.

The truth is Esther could have any number of fellas, but she only wants one.

'Do you think I'll see you know who tonight?', she whispers with a wink.

'I haven't seen Daniel lately', Nanny says as she leans over to poke the fire.

'No', Esther says, barely audible, pretending to look for something in her bag.

'Don't you run after him; do you hear me? You let him alone, if he wants you, he'll find you, do you hear me?', Nanny says, standing with her back to the fire, rubbing her legs.

'I know, I won't, I won't', Esther says, her cheeks momentarily flushed bright pink.

'I love you Esther', I tell her as she walks out the door.

'I love you too', she says as she turns back to me.

'That's lovely on you. Go on now, they're waiting on you', my Nanny shoos her out the door, but watches her silently, helplessly from the front window. Shuffling by me, she interrupts her conversation with herself and asks me: 'Do you want a cup a tea and a tomatta sandwich?'

17

The room is as black as the wardrobe in the wall when I hid in it ... in the middle of the night Esther's sobs wake me up as she climbs onto the top bunk above me. 'Why are you cryin' I ask her.

'Shush go back to sleep ... '

The next morning, the coalman, tall, with powdered black and red, sweat-streaked face, dumps a bag of coal into the box in the coalhouse.

He is one of the biggest men I've ever seen, and he looks like an Indian chief to me. His bright blue eyes shine from his dark rimmed lids; 'That's it, Esther just one bag, is it?'

'Yeh, thanks very much', Esther hands him a crisp five Punt note.

'Thanks that's great, I'll see you next week. Tell Willie I was asking for him, will you?', he says as he shuts the front door behind him.

'I will God Bless.' Esther checks it's locked, then looks at the trail of coal dust from the little hall into the living room; 'He's a lovely fella but every week he destroys me floors. Aw but he's harmless. He's a lovely chap, wouldn't do you a bad turn. Get me the brush', she sweeps the offending floor then lifts the dust with the small shovel she gets in the coalhouse (under the stairs), then throws it on the insipid fire. The coal was emptied into a large wooden box with a small opening at the bottom, enough for a small shovel to collect the coal. She only closed the coalhouse door when we heard the gate squeak; 'Who's that? Look quick', she tells me.

'It's Daniel', I tell her, 'Will I open the door?', my trick to stand on the hall table and open the door made everyone who called by laugh.

'No wait, wait till he knocks' with that, she dashes into the bathroom and re-appears in a pretty pink jumper, runs to the sink, throws water on her face and hands, wipes them in the tea towel and runs to the side of the stereo. He's still knocking as she grabs the brush and pulls it through her hair.

'I'm coming, I'm coming.' She rushes past me, throws the brush behind the couch, stands for a second, takes a breath, and then opens the door.

'How are yeh, come in? She puts her right hand through her hair and saunters to the kitchen, like the cat that got the cream; 'Do you want a cup of tea, it's made?', she says.

'Yes, I'd love one', he says taking off his suit jacket, then holds it up, folds it over, catches the crease mark on the sleeves, folds them over again, then places it over the back of the armchair, like it's the only jacket he ever had or will have again. The armchair at the window in the front room faces the tiny kitchen.

'Do you want a sandwich, or cake, a biscuit, I've a lovely Victoria Sponge there me Mammy bought in Mannings?', she says leaning over the counter that separates both rooms.

'No, no thank you, my mother has my dinner on for me. How are you? How've you been ... '

'I, I'm sorry for the way I acted for what I said. You've always been the best in the world to me. I was wrong I shouldn't have said that.'

'It's ok, no harm done Esther, I'm always here for you, we've always been friends, I ... how's your mother? Hiya Sheila, that's a lovely doll', he says. I nod in acknowledgement and smile but continue with the business of dressing my baby doll in her new outfit. I don't really like him, but I don't really know why. He's always nice to me, and when they took me to the zoo, he bought me a glass sugar red soother.

'Me Mammy's great, I ... , she's out selling. I'm doing great; Sally Murphy's getting me a new job in the chocolate factory at the back of South Circular Road. The money's good and I don't have to work the weekends.' Esther tells him.

'Oh, that's great, it's only down the road. You look well', he says as he takes the rattling cup and saucer, that she hardly ever uses, from her hands.

'I haven't seen you in ages. I thought you'd be around. Vera got engaged. I called around to your mothers to invite you, but she said you were gone out with Maura. Your Mammy was very rude to me. I was very hurt Daniel.' she tells him.

'I thought it was best to let things lie; she told me you called. I'm sorry about that. I don't know why she, anyway, Esther, I'm sorry she did that she'd no business of telling you, saying that' he says, bristling.

'I ... I thought you said you loved me ... you said, I believed you ... ', Esther's voice quivers as she stands in the middle of the room; she looks much younger than she is, petite in her pink jumper and white three-quarter length trousers.

'I do, I always will, but as a friend, I told you that; I thought you understood. We're better off as friends, I don't ... do you understand?', he says.

'I understand, I understand ... is that her name, Maura is she, where's she from, Dublin?', Esther asks him as she wipes a cloth over the clean kitchen table for the third time.

'No, she's from the country, Kilkenny; she's a schoolteacher. She's just started at Terenure College, it's a private school. She's really nice; you'd like her', his words slow and cruel; the pride he basks in, conceited.

'Is she, good for her ... I've to get ready. I'm going out. Do you want more tea before you go?' Esther's tone changes with the crimson flash of her cheeks.

'Eh no, no thanks, you going somewhere nice?', he asks.

'I'm going out with someone; you don't know him', she says, flicking her hair.

'Oh, good, good ... Are you going to Madge's birthday? I'll see you there. Will I? Are you coming? Will I see, see you, you there?', he stutters.

'You might. I don't know, I mightn't go, I'll see', she says, clearing the cup and saucer in between him taking sips of the tea he hasn't finished. She then marches to the kitchen, and turns the taps on fully, so she can't hear what he's saying, causing the water to splash into the basin and all around the sink.

'Right Esther', he says to her back, 'I'll see you Saturday then.'

'Wha?', she says.

He shouts louder, his face contorted, he doesn't like to shout; 'I said, I'll see you Saturday then?'

'Oh, I said you might, I said', she raises her voice.

'Ok, I'll see you Saturday', he says and doesn't move.

'Right!', she shouts, then under her breath whispers, 'I said you might.'

21

He hears her and shakes his head; 'Good night.' he tells her, quietly closing the door behind him as he leaves.

And with the click of the latch, she falls to the floor. The water still running, is splashing everywhere, including on my head. The wet cloth in her hand soaks the press, as it slides down it. She lies forward sobbing into her hands, the cloth by now sitting in a puddle on the lino beside her.

'Are you ok Esther, it's ok don't cry', I eventually hear my voice.

She holds on to the sink with both hands and pulls herself up, leans over it and silently rocks, tears streaming from her eyes. 'He's not coming back to me ... he's not coming back to me, oh, I thought he was coming to get back with me, oh Mammy ... ' she cries; the sound, a deep moaning I've never heard before.

I hold on to her leg and rub her hand 'It's ok, are you ok now?'

'Yes, I'm, it's ok ... ', she eventually answers. 'Here an I get you a bar a chocolate ... I'll put on *Heidi* for you ... '

Her voice sounds like mine when I had a sore throat and didn't go to school for two weeks. She wipes her face in a towel and then throws it into the sink, 'Come on, you sit there, and I'll put on the dinner.' I sit and watch *Heidi*, but my time with the little Swiss is intermittently interrupted by sobs from the kitchen.

'Don't tell your Nanny I was crying; sure you won't, promise me?', she tells me over the counter.

'No' I tell her, and I didn't.

My Mother's House

I'm home again in my mother's house and going to big school now, though at weekends and holidays I stay with Nanny and Esther.

'Sheila Hamilton get into the bold corner', says Bridie Power, the tall, dark handsome teacher who runs the school near our house.

I spend a lot of time in the 'bold corner.' This entails facing a blue wall for long periods of time. I am usually put in this corner for a list of serious offences including hitting other children, cheeking teachers, using 'bad' language and the very odd time, spitting at another child! My mortified mother tries to explain that my behaviour is a result of her in-laws allowing me to run wild. However, it isn't all bad, as regular requests from my teachers for me to sing and dance are met with rapturous applause and as many *Blue Ribbon* chocolate bars as I can stuff in my face.

Esther and my Nanny are a captive audience when I sing, dance, and direct them to move furniture, set up stage and clap on command. Mostly willing participants, they shower me with compliments and applause.

But occasionally my exuberance breaks their benevolent spirits and erodes their tolerance.

'That's enough now, ye have to stop, sit down, sit down. Sit down, I said!'

But overall, they indulge me as the star, I think I am. My mother, on the other hand, is not so tolerant. I am now a background dancer in a chorus of four children (eventually six), my two older brothers, are my comrades/ heroes, my younger and only sister, Carly, is my friend. My mother is now a thirty-year-old, bohemian 'housewife', as contradictory and conflicted a term as she is herself.

She's a creative kaleidoscope, a painter, writer, designer, dressmaker, baker, gardener, and artist. When free and unrestrained, she's a firefly that lights up and sprinkles her magic particles everywhere she goes, but for now, she's a free spirit confined by motherhood and frustrated by a misaligned education. She wanted to go to art college; but her mother insisted on secretarial, she herself a tailor, had worked 'too hard', and wanted an easier life for her daughter. This was an irreconcilable misalliance of artist and medium. This conflict would not be rectified until my mother, like a caterpillar, cast off her ever-restraining shackles, flew into the warm sun and basked in a coloured eutopia that nature unleashed in all its glory. At forty two she began to paint again, but for now, she is steering this ship, and mostly alone. Her daily chores, 'woman's work' are solely hers. She could be tired, sick, weary, sad, frustrated, heartbroken or angry, which she sometimes is, but this show had to go on.

She is wonderful, fun, irreverent, disorganised, unortho-dox, oddball, alternative, she doesn't so much break the rules as completely ignore them. She's incredibly generous of spirit, minds no one's business but her own, is kind, caring and wonderfully bonkers.

She walks in the rain, makes a mess, sews costumes, dances in the kitchen, bakes cakes, plays in puddles, raises dogs, cats, hamsters and budgies. She swims in seas, walks in mountains, picks blackberries, gives away everything, rolls down hills, cycles our bikes, leads our adventures, and brings us on holidays.

When pushed, she shouts, scolds, throws clocks, shoes, insults, dishes, and tantrums. 'I should have put yis in an orphanage and abandoned yis like your father did, yis ungrateful shower of bastards!' As she slams her door, seismic rumbles shake the very foundation of our home. These moments, when she loses her temper, rare and volcanic. In a house that eludes silence, there is suddenly an intrepid calm. Even the dog, nervous and wary, doesn't leave his trench but keeps watch at a safe distance. His eyes barely raised above the parapet of his bed as he carefully monitors the speed, weight, intensity and comings and goings of her footsteps.

She can spend money like a Rockefeller. Toys, treats, takeaways, cream cakes, money, whatever us kids want, whenever we want it. Come the morning, she hasn't a penny for the school bus fares. Drawers, presses, sideboards, couches, and cushions are unceremoniously upended, while pockets are turned inside out and rifled for loose change. She blares Clifford T. Ward, Carly Simon, The Rolling Stones, Cat Stevens, Johnny Mathis and many more great artists.

Odd socks and a uniform half creased, 'The heat of your body will take them out', she stalls the bus while we run for it one by one.

My father supplies ample amounts of money every Friday, and every week without fail she runs out of it. And so, it's a source of constant amusement to us children that he is continually surprised by my mother's spending;

'Where's the money I gave you Friday?', my father's off!

'Gone', my mother's haughty response.

My father's hands up in the air now, 'Gone, gone again! Just like that, GONE! Sweet Jesus, Mary and Joseph, The Shah of Iran couldn't keep you in money! This is terrible, I couldn't keep this up, all I'm doing is giving you money and you haven't a penny again! Aw this is terrible.' He then turns to us kids and repeats a line we've heard a thousand times; 'Do you know your mother only saved a fiver for our wedding, do yis? A fiver! I'm going to work!'

When my mother bakes, the kitchen, though spotless when she begins, is left in a catastrophic state, and a light dusting of flour covers the whole house. The smell of her baking is the scent of sweet ecstasy. The taste of her apple tarts with cream immobilises me into a rapturous state. The pots, pans, bowls, dishes, mixers are piled high in the sink like a tipsy trophy to her most recent endeavour. She isn't what you'd call house proud, but anyone who tasted her upside-down pineapple sponge cake with custard would never mind.

The smell of soup, piled plates of sliced corned beef, ham, haslet, cheddar cheese, *Brennan's* bread and turnover fills the cosy room. My father tears into our front kitchen in the basement of the three-story broken-down house with his employees in tow. He jumps down our dark, worn back stairs three steps at a time. Lean, good-looking, red hair, high cheekbones and always in a hurry. In come big men, big boots, warm dusty hands, stained work clothes with their old school manners, embarrassed to invade my mother's kitchen. My father shouts his demands, 'Make the lads sandwiches Bette, bowls a soup there Bette ... Kids get their lunch Bette? Did you type those estimates Bette? Need them today, Bette. Need cheques by Friday Bette.'

Easy going and great fun, most days, she makes the sandwiches, serves the soup, stews the tea, makes the dinner, washes clothes, does the shopping, pulls hair into ponytails, does our homework. If we're too tired and its bedtime, or in the morning or if we're late, she finishes our homework for us with whatever instrument is at hand, biro, pencil, or crayon. She's not fussy and scrolls across the pages in her big, generous, attached hand, then signs it. 'Now, it's done, don't be worrying.' She laughs when told of the frustrated teacher hurling the copy book (sometimes with a jam sandwich attached) across the room. Every evening, she types estimates till past midnight and watches as her husband gets ready to go out at seven, sharp.

As the spring bulbs force their heads through stiffened soil, I climb the dark back stairs of our old house. I keep my left hand on the bannisters as my right sweeps the gloss-painted wallpaper on the ancient tenement walls. The paper so heavy and thick with layers of stiff paint, that it hangs and greets me at intervals, so eager is it to tell the story of every tenant family that shared the rooms in our bedraggled house. The hall is lit up, the cutting spring bright sunshine pierces through the open door and squints my eyes, forcing one to close and the other to see through what looks to me like a shimmering, glistening spider's web. Mesmerised, I stand dazed.

'Be careful; hold the railings coming down, good girl',

my mother pats the warm granite shimmering step for me to sit beside her.

The tiny mint green flowers on her soft navy shirt, dance and bounce off the emerald in her shining, bashful lashed, almond-shaped eyes. A brown tweed hacking jacket warms the side of my head in the virgin sun, casually glamourous and accompanied by a flowing rust skirt; her brown knee-high soft leather boots are crossed and swinging. She's sitting on the steps outside our house. She lifts her glasses to wipe away the tears streaming down her face.

'Are you crying Mammy?', I ask. 'No', she nods and pats my ribbed tighted leg. 'I'm laughing!'

Kathleen, our neighbour, throws her head back showing her thick white teeth, as she exhales a gust of smoke at the same time. She to me, looks like a movie star.

'Imagine, her throwing the tin of peas over the wall and nearly knocking him out. Well, what he's not after calling her, isn't worth mentioning!' Kathleen is now lying on the concrete steps, stretched out laughing, sunburnt and brown, like a Cherokee on sacred resting ground. She then bolts upright, choking on her own throaty laugh.

My mother's skin so scrunched, her glasses fall off their peak. Her freckles, usually on a tan display, disappear into the wrinkles on her nose. Her bronzed cheeks flush with sun glaze and coral blossom; her blooming lips pulled across a white ivory cave. Her mostly soft laugh, silent except for at the end of each forward motion there escapes a long high pitched, squeal, revealing a smile so wide I can see her dainty back teeth.

She possesses the rarest of jewels; a reserved, sultry natural charm. Like a trinket swinging from a chain, with the slightest twist, it sparkles and stuns.

My mother is still wiping the tears from her eyes when she, after several attempts finally asks, 'Why, why did Dympna throw the tin of peas over the wall?'

Kathleen, with the tips of her fingers, rubs the raven eye liner escaped from the slits of her handsome feline eyes; 'To warn Mary that the gas man was coming to check the metres. Tony from out the back was after rigging the central metre and they were sending an engineer because we're all getting free gas. Wasn't Eddy home sick fixing a truck out the back when Mary called him in for his lunch? He was walking through the yard and got a smack of the tin a peas in the head! Mary is after running into my kitchen on her hands and knees laughing. I thought she was going to wet herself, the two of us were watching him out the window. Well, the names he's after calling poor Dympna, and she only trying to warn us.'

'Does she usually throw tins across the wall?', my mother asks incredulously, still laughing at the thought.

'Ah no, not usually tins, it's usually a stone or bit a coal she throws at the back door. You know to warn Mary if the milkman or coalman's comin to get paid.' Realising the absurdity of what she is saying, Kathleen, pauses for a moment, then they both howl, laughing again.

On days like this the world is a warm and fuzzy place. Our neighbours are our friends, and we love them. 'Run in and ask Kathleen for a drop a milk. Ask Marie for a cup of sugar. Run down and ask Auntie May for the loan of a darning needle so I can finish your jumper.'

My mother has the resources but mostly can't be bothered with the finer details of domesticity. My father has a habit of buying her household appliances to assist her in her tasks. He only shuts the front door behind him, when she opens the back one, and flings the offending object at the back wall; 'That's what I think of that! Suit him better to stay in one night and help me!' Her carefree nature shrouds a resilience that is her saving grace, as at her young age, she's already experienced her fair share of heartache.

My father is now back with his family, us, having up and gone to San Francisco on one of his 'business trips', whilst my mother was pregnant, having lost her mother only 11 months before.

Nelly

In a world of summer holidays, sunshine, sweets, cakes, frilly dresses, singing, dancing, cousins and garden picnics, Nelly is the bane of my life. She lives at the end of my Nanny's road, before the bridge. So, wherever we go, to the church, shop, butchers or town we have to pass Nelly's house.

Nelly is tall, thin, with rotten teeth and a long masculine jaw. She wears a blue coat, a pale blue headscarf tied so tightly under her chin it's a wonder she isn't decapitated! Her wiry grey hair escapes and sprigs from her collar. She has big, wicked black circled eyes and a sharp, lop-sided nose. She is in her mid-fifties and absolutely terrifies me. Even at just six years old, I can sense this creature is unhinged, and dangerous. She walks like a rabid dog, wild, determined, and ready to turn. The odd time she calls to my Nanny's door and asks for an apple, I run, tremble, and hide under the stairs. My Nanny, kindness itself, gives her a bag of them. Nelly likes my Nanny and always answers her with a 'Thanks Mrs', but she loathes my auntie Esther and has made a run at her before.

You see, Nelly has an unhealthy obsession with my auntie's friend Timmy Murphy and is convinced Esther is trying to take him from her. There is no truth whatsoever to this. Timmy is the very married proprietor of the local shop on the corner of the South Circular Road and has a wife called Anita, a seamstress who works upstairs and has 'a tongue that could strip paint.' Esther is her good friend and customer. Anita has 'no time for girls', but she says she doesn't mind me as, according to her, I'm cheeky like herself.

The first time I remember climbing Anita's creaking, crooked, back stairs, I was four years old. When the door opened, it revealed a girly wonderland. The most beautiful fabrics, ribbons, petticoats, dresses, and skirts were hung, flung and draped everywhere in the tiny room. That Easter, she made me the most beautiful white cotton and lemon dress; it had puff sleeves, a beautiful ribbon and a full petticoat, which I liked the best.

Timmy's shop is a bursting, frantic, mini metropolis, where groceries, meat, clothes, and electronics are bought, sold, and traded. Some of which were rescued from or fell off the back of a lorry, depending on your perspective! A place where drop-offs have no dockets and customers get no receipts. Where cash is the currency, and your word is your bond.

I am back in my grandmother's house for the summer holidays and spend most afternoons playing with my cousins and listening to my aunt's incessant chatter. All seven of them sharing second-hand cigarette smoke, cakes, gossip and news of market bargains. This particular Saturday they are discussing who got what at the Liberty Market, and for how much. This was a source of constant exhilaration and sometimes irritation and all depended on the identity of the procurer. The market in Meath Street, a collection of *ad hoc* stalls. A haphazard, chaotic shanty that sold the most beautiful bags, coats, clothes, hats and shoes. A close family member or well-liked person's haul was received with an 'Aw jaysus it's only massive', 'Gorgeous'.

'That's for nuthin'.

'They gave dat away'.

'That's beautiful on ya!'

However, if the buyer, was not liked; 'A consequence', 'Mean' or a 'Dose', her gains were met with much hostility and a range of responses from the subdued to direct; 'That's nice.' or 'Oh did she?'. 'That's not like her to buy clothes?'. 'She has her communion money'. If the culprit was truly despised a 'Hungry c**t, wouldn't spend Christmas!', could be slipped in under a breath.

The pristine hall, with its dark wine-flowered carpet and crooked telephone table that teeters on the brink, is hoovered daily. The cream woodchipped walls provide me with a head office/playground. The stairs steep and barely wide enough for two small bodies, hold children's races. The aim to go down headfirst from top to bottom, without knocking yourself out!

In my world, my dolls are my own business and not to be shared. I line them up on the stairs for all to observe. A bewildered, beautiful and silent army guarded by me, from outstretched arms, snotty noses and teary eyes.

'Ah give her a shot of your doll, will you let her hold it?', cajoles my auntie Esther.

'No,' was my immediate and emphatic response. Most days, I get to do what I like without interference. We play music, sing, dance, eat sweets, put on makeup, go to mass, watch *Dallas*, *Worzel*, *Scooby Doo*, *Heidi* and go shopping. Esther gets scolded regularly, because of me; 'You have her ruined', 'You spoil that young one, no wonder she won't do what she's told', 'You have her the way she is.'

Esther fires back rapidly; 'Mind your own business!', 'Nothing to do with you!', 'Leave her alone!' All that said, on days like Saturdays, there is more than one commander, so I have to be careful. A bridge too far and threats of my legs being 'reddened' are bandied around.

Esther tries again, 'Ah look at her, poor Imelda, she's crying, let her hold the doll. Please for me, just for one minute.' An instruction from the front room is shouted out loudly; 'Let her play with it, don't be so bold.'

'No!', I decide to dig in my heels. After all, it wasn't their house, and besides, Esther wouldn't make me. She winks at me, 'Ah, will you let her play with it?', then whispers, 'I'll let you stay up late tonight and buy you wine gums?'

Done! Temporarily overcome with magnanimity at the thought of wine gums, and subject to the ongoing tongue-lashing from the other room. I relent and let my crying cousin, for a short time, hold my doll, and then promptly whip it away. She howls tears of tempered sorrow and screams, 'Maaaammy!' Her mother, my older aunt's furious face, appears around the door, ready to do a job on me, when the door knocker crashes, clanks, bangs. The thick heavy mahogany front door shudders, and the glass rattles nervously in the frame.

My aunt stunned at the force of this knock, opens the door slowly.

'Is your Mammy there?', the voice is familiar, singing, taunting, slow with a half-baked faked innocence. This same familiarity brings Esther to the door; 'Yeh, what do you want?'

'I wasn't talking to you', the voice claps back. 'I want your mother.' Her tone tries to mask her desperation, aggression. Her madness chills me to the core.

'Well, she's not here I said.' Esther, brave and tiny, slams the door in her face. My aunts, in unison, gasp in disgust; 'Aw Estherrrr!!! Who was that?'

'Nelly', she answers.

'Ah God love her! What did she want?' 'Ah that's terrible!', 'You shouldn't have done that?' 'That's not nice.' 'The poor woman's harmless', they scold Esther. Esther distractedly walks back to her armchair, hogging the right side of the brass framed fire. 'Harmless me arse, she pulled a knife on me two weeks ago in Timmy Murphy's shop. Told me she'd slit me throat. Timmy had to calm her down.' The crowd gasps again, and the room rains questions. By now, I'd abandoned all thoughts of my unchaperoned possessions as horror struck my very being at the very mention of that unholy name.

I grab Esther's arm 'Was it her? Was it? Was it Nelly? Was it her, Esther?' I stand at the side of her chair shaking, clutching her sleeve, eyes wide open.

Esther pushes out a laugh and fixes the lemon bow in my hair; 'Don't mind her, Nelly with the rubber belly. She won't be saying a word to you, I'll give her a kick in the arse for herself.' I read her steely blue eyes. I could trust Esther, she never lied to me. Well, only when she got all dressed up with makeup and told me she'd be 'Back in a minute.' I cried without her, but she did come back, laughing, singing too loud and unable to walk straight. Nanny said she was ashamed of her life. But Nelly! Esther would never lie about Nelly!

'Nelly took my money and shouted at me in the shop. Remember Esther? I'm afraid!', water sits in my eyes. I panic, my mind races. What ifs, fly around my head like wasps in a sweetshop window. Overwhelmed, I sink into her shoulder and cry. But before I completely disintegrate into a puddle of tears, my wonderful aunts gather around and console me. They jokingly raise fists, wring hands, and give it to Nelly in the proverbial neck!

'Who shouted at you, who took your money?', said one.

'I'll break her face!', said the other.

They all join in; 'The cheek of her, how dare she!', 'No one's putting a hand on you', 'Wait till I get me hands on her!', 'The dirty bitch!' I can't help but giggle and laugh and although not totally free of my horror, I'm much relieved. In the foggy, overcrowded, coddle-smelling front room, I know in that moment, that they love me.

My run-in with Nelly took place the previous Sunday evening. Nanny had gone to bingo and Esther was sniffling quietly in the corner. Lately, she was doing this a lot. She said she saw 'You know who' up at the doctor with his mother; 'He barely said hello to me. Don't tell your Nanny, but I called round to his house again. That oul bitch of a mother of his, answered the door and told me he was gone out. Out WITH MAURA. I haven't eaten a thing since. I keep praying they'll break up, that he'll come back to me. God forgive me!'

'He will, he will, I'll say a prayer too', I promise her, sure no one could ever not come back to her. Of that, I was certain. I didn't like it when she was like this, it made me feel sad and want to go home to my mother's house.

'Are you sad?', I ask her.

'No, there's something in me eye. I'm ok now', interrupted by one last sniffle and dabbed by a well-wrung tissue, her eyes light up with a smile; 'Will I bring you for an ice cream?'

I nod yes and pleased with myself, I show her the fifty-pence piece my Daddy gave me; 'I'll buy us ice creams today!'

'Oh lovely!', she says, picking herself up and walking to the kitchen; 'You're very good. Now, will you run up and get me a clean facecloth out of the wardrobe in the wall?'

It had been a hot and sticky day filled with loneliness and an empty house. The kind of day when it's beautiful outside, and everyone is all dressed up and has somewhere to go. Well, we had nowhere to go, nowhere but to Timmy Murphy's shop to buy ice creams. As we close the rickety red gate behind us, it is now a glorious balmy evening. I'm happy as we saunter down the road, exchanging greetings with our neighbours and strangers along the way.

'Goin out Mary? You look great.'

'Beauriful evenin Esther.'

'Lovely night, isn't it?'

'Night and God bless,' was my very favourite. I thought it was very kind of neighbours and strangers, alike, to bless us, so at regular intervals, I returned the blessing to people I liked the look of; 'Night an God Bless you' I tell them until Esther laughs out loud and tells me to stop.

The beautiful sky whips up a pale pink, peach dessert as I skip towards a strawberry, chocolate *Cornetto*. On entering Timmy Murphy's shop, I am stopped in my tracks, for there in front of me, is Nelly hovering around the counter.

'I said he's too busy. Now for the last time, you'll have to make do with me.', Eileen, a regal redhead and Timmy's sister, chastises Nelly. Nelly, annoyed and agitated, says she'll wait for Timmy, then circles herself, muttering obscenities. Tugging at her scarf, she reminds me of a mad bird I once saw, plucking its own feathers.

Eileen motions me to come nearer the counter. Carefully I take my fifty-pence piece from my beaded pink purse and put it on the counter.

With that, I feel a tap on my shoulder; 'Hello', it's Timmy. He came through the front door dressed in his white shop coat and went behind the counter.

'Who's next?', he says.

Nelly jumps forward; 'Me! How are you, Timmy?', she says. 'I want two slices of corned beef Timmy', blushing as she counts out half pennies, pennies and two pence pieces.

'It's for me brother', she volunteers. Timmy wraps the two slices and hands her an open piece of brown paper with a few more slices on top; 'They're for you.' Without even looking up Nelly grabs the brown paper and pushes the content into her face. She gets most of it into her mouth, and the few scraps that fall on her arm, she snaps up and eats.

'Now, what will I get you?', he turns to me. I was about to tell him when I realise my money is no longer where I'd left it. My heart sinks. 'Me money, me money is gone. I put it there' and point to the top of the counter straight ahead.

'Are you sure?', Timmy asks, 'There's nothing there. Are you sure, check your pockets?'

'I put it there', I say as I hand him my purse full of coins. 'I only had one 50p piece, me Daddy gave me.' With that, and out of the blue, Nelly's voice pierces the air, she's shouting at me, 'It wasn't me; I didn't take it!! I never touched it! It wasn't me.' The image of her long, wiry right hand sliding on the counter and covering my coin flashes before my eyes. Right then and there, I knew she had taken it. I had seen her do it.

Frozen with fright, I hear Esther's voice. She was outside talking to Eileen; 'Who are you talkin to like that? Don't shout at her, I'm warning you. Who do you think you're talkin to?'

Nelly is getting more and more agitated when Timmy finally raises his voice 'Stop Nelly. You are not to do that again, now I'm warning you! She's only a child. Now I'm telling you. Stop shouting. Do you hear me?'

Nelly, cute as a fox, answers like a lamb, 'I won't. I'm sorry Timmy. I'll never do it again. I didn't take it. I didn't take her money.'

Eileen out of her smock and shining like a Christmas bauble chimes in, too. 'You do that again Nelly, and I will bar you. Are you alright honey? Night Esther, see you tomorrow.'

Things had cooled down when Timmy went to the freezer to get me an ice cream. But just as he turned his back, Nelly smirked at me with a side eye and stuck her lizard tongue out. I felt my blood rise, frustrated by fear, tears, and temper. Unaware my words had the breath or courage to carry them. I shouted at her; 'You took it! I saw you! You took my money! I saw her do it.' Having stunned everyone in the room, including myself, I immediately, deeply, bitterly, and sorely regretted my outburst. For there in front of me was Nelly going berserk. Flinging her arms in the air, jumping up and down. Her knees touching her chin.

She was screaming and dancing in front of me like Rumpelstiltskin from my Ladybird storybook. He had terrorised me too.

She was shouting at me now, her big eyes touching my lashes, though I didn't hear a word she said so immobilised was I with fright.

Then suddenly, I was jerked out of my daze. She grabbed me by both shoulders and proceeded to shake me. Esther snapped me out of her hands and pushed her; 'Don't you dare put your hands on her; I'll break you're effing face for you. I'll get the police for you! Don't you dare touch her! I'm warning you!'

Timmy ran from behind the counter. 'You're out', he shouted at Nelly, 'Now that's it! You're barred! Get out! That's the end of it now. The last straw! I am not having that! Out! Get out and stay out!!!'

Nelly wailed like the Banshee outside a dying window as she pointed at me. She screeched, moaned and pleaded with Timmy, 'It's her fault. I didn't do anything wrong. I didn't do it!' He was having none of it. She was still pointing at me as he pushed her out the door. 'I'll get you for this! I'll get ya!', she said from outside the shop.

'That's enough Nelly!', Timmy demanded. 'Go on. Go on now. Go home!'

Timmy's face was as white as the ice cream he gave me,

'She's gone. Are you alright chicken? Here now, there's a lovely ice cream. She's gone. It's ok.' I wasn't hungry anymore; I was shaking, hysterical and clinging to Esther. I didn't want the ice cream. The bottom had fallen out of my stomach and my world. I was so overcome with fear that I could hardly put one foot in front of the other. Esther was shaking too. As we scurried over the bridge, the darkness smothered us like a saturated blanket. Just as we got to the end of the small craggy bridge wall, we spotted a blackened figure leaning over it. Esther pulled me into the middle of the road and told me to hurry. As we ran by, a drunkard swung around, with an empty bottle in his hand and burst into a belligerent rendition of '*Molly Malone*.' I didn't like it, but I wasn't the only one. Esther was nervous of drunkards and nightfall too. She clutched my hand even tighter.

The deserted road now echoed with the hurried clicks of our shoes. The houses, dark and relentless, stretched ahead on both sides of the abandoned street. I wore my white clogs which slipped off my heels and hurt when I walked too fast. The cantankerous, meandering streetlights cast shadow and light when they felt like it. More often than not, they denied their glow.

'It's dark out. I'm afraid, Esther', I moaned. She pulled me under her light pink sports jacket, 'You're ok; we'll be home soon. Don't worry.'

I didn't spot Nelly until we passed her gate. It clanked so hard I clutched Esther and yelped at the same time. 'Fuckin bitch', she hissed as she stood welded to the ground glaring at us.

'Who are you talking to? Wait till I see Timmy Murphy

tomorrow! I'll tell him how sorry you are. You keep it up, and I'll get the police for you!', Esther yelled as we rushed by. Nelly stood defiant, then strolled to her grey, dilapidated door with the mucky net curtains that hadn't seen water since they were thrown up. There, she leaned and watched us. Lurking in the shadows. Even the raven night couldn't conceal her wicked eyeballs. From that day on, she was the subject of my nightmares. I was beyond relieved to see my Nanny when we got home. There she was on the couch having her night-time snack of bread, butter, and tea.

I hurriedly told her what Nelly had done to me. Esther continued the story when I ran out of breath, but Nanny didn't even look up. Instead, she nodded as she took large bites of bread, leaving her false teeth marks in the quarter inch of butter that plastered it. I stood in silence, confused. I was waiting on her to tell me about what she was going to do to Nelly. Nothing. Then, when she'd gulped a mouthful of tea to wash down her supper, she finally spoke, 'Esther you shouldn't be tormenting that poor woman; she's not right. She lives with her brother. Mr Kavanagh says he takes her money and he's cruel to her. I know all about you tormentin her. Telling her you're Timmy Murphy's girlfriend. You ought to be ashamed of yourself! You leave that woman alone!'

Esther protested, 'I only said it once, and besides, it was a joke. She pulled a knife on me Mammy! And as for Mr Kavanagh, the merry widower, he doesn't need the blessed virgin to comfort him anymore, cos I seen him walking hand in hand with Mrs Conway!'

'You mind your own business, Mr Kavanagh is a

gentleman and broke his heart over his poor wife passing, and as for Nelly, I don't want to hear that woman's name mentioned again! That woman's not well!'

Well, of all the disappointments I'd ever experienced this was the worst! I couldn't believe my ears.

Nanny didn't even look up! Nor call Nelly one name, nor threaten to get her, kill her, maim her, nothing! I was so upset that I went to bed without being told to and cried bitter tears until my pillow was damp. I couldn't believe it. What a let-down my Nanny was.

Esther shook as she got into the moonlit top bunk in the box room; 'It's cold tonight. Did you wear your bed socks?'

'If Nelly kills me tomorrow, it's me Nanny's fault. I'm never speaking to her again. I hate her. She doesn't care about me and I'm tellin me Daddy on her and I'm going home and never coming back' I whisper to Esther.

Esther, weary, tries to appease me. 'Ah don't say that Nanny didn't mean it. Nanny loves you. She won't let Nelly say a word to you, I promise. Stop crying now and go to sleep; you're tired. We're going to the beach in the morning with auntie Phil and the girls. You'll have a lovely day.'

So battered were my spirits and ravaged was my heart that I couldn't even muster an obligatory 'No!'

Body of Christ

I was so seriously aggrieved by my Nanny's distasteful and unforeseen conduct over Nelly, I settled on ignoring her for at least six months. But relented on the first day when she offered to take me out selling, to the market, to her friends, and then to the slots. Most importantly, it meant a large *Knicker Bocker Glory* in Thomas Street on the way home.

Esther still went down to Timmy Murphy's shop but tried to avoid Nelly. I chose not to go at all. Instead, whenever I wanted sweets, we went to Mr Forshaw's corner shop as he, by now, was my main supplier. Mr Forshaw's corner shop was perched on the opposite side of Sally's Bridge.

A visit to this establishment was a divine assault on one's senses. The sweetest smells perfumed the air, while glass jars of rainbow-coloured sweets oozed from shelves and electrified my mind. So close, but so tauntingly far away. Overwhelmed, I'd almost faint with the dizzying excitement of choosing which jar would furnish me with its exquisite delights.

There was no wiggle room for bad behaviour with Mr Forshaw, though I was willing to endure his greased black hair, tombstone teeth and freezing cold stare to get my just desserts. He was a towering, laterally immense man, who moved methodically and slowly. He would open the red-topped glass jar I had chosen and eyeball me as the sweets plopped onto the weighing scales. The sound of cola cubes, pear drops, wine gums or bon bons, ping, plop, plop, plop, ping as they drop to the metal bowl on the weighing scales. 'A quarter?', he bellows in his Northern English accent. The exchange was quick. With a nod and a skip, I pick up my sweets and run.

Heaven is in a brown paper bag. If the sweets are hard, I try to suck them until they are small, but I never get very far. I bite, crash and smash through the glass and swallow them one after another. Sometimes, a *Lemon* or *Strawberry Sherbert* might release a fizz surprise, or a quarter of *Bon Bons* might tire my jaws.

I enjoy immensely the sensation of stuffing half the bag of jellies into my mouth. Overloaded on divine delirium, I hope I won't choke, all the while trying not to walk the lines on the pavement, which became a mild obsession, as did trying to avoid Nelly.

Most of the time, we manage just fine and cross the road to the other side before we get to Nelly's house. I insist on this diversion. But sometimes Nelly sees us crossing the road and screams after us, 'Esther, you bitch you, you keep away from Timmy Murphy, I'm warning you.' Esther turns to me and whispers, 'Ah shut up Nelly with the rubber belly', and we run down the road - Esther laughing, me shaking.

Even these occasions became less frequent. It seems Nelly had finally let the whole money in the shop incident go. And besides, I was older now by nearly a whole year and understood what Nanny said about Nelly not being well. I had also long forgiven Nanny for her behaviour and even helped around the house. I particularly liked summer mornings when the door was open, and music was playing, Patsy Cline, Hot Chocolate or Dolly Parton rocking the show, Esther cleaning. This was a very serious operation. Chairs turned upside down, tables, ornaments, and furniture moved. Buckets, old rags, newspapers, mops, brushes, soft and hard, bleach, furniture polish, Brasso, window cleaner and disinfectant. Gathered and ready for action.

When I could be bothered, my job was to lift the mats from the hall and front step and throw them across the hedge. Or fetch and carry supplies from the backyard to the front and scrub the steps when Esther let me. Though sometimes I took liberties with the washing up liquid and water and made a mess.

'Now that's lovely. Give me the bucket.'

'But I'm helping you. I want to do it', me, refusing to give it over.

'You're destroying the place! You've the floors soaking wet! Here,' Esther hands me a Turkish Delight, her favourite, 'Now sit there and eat that.'

I often insist on making her and Nanny eggs on toast. Though it means Nanny or Esther have to get out of bed to turn on the gas. 'Get up Nanny. I want to make you breakfast', I tell her.

'I'm not hungry yet', Nanny mumbles. What time is it, 7 o'clock! Sweet Mary, Jesus and Joseph isn't this inhuman. Esther, tell that young one to stop! It's too early! Go back to sleep!' Nanny's eyes are squinting at her clock. Grandad sleeps in the spare room because of his shiftwork, and besides he doesn't like breakfast, but does smoke at least seventeen cigarettes in the morning

(I counted) with his pot of tea that looks like black tar!

'I'm hungry!', I insist. This is a ploy to get my own way and Nanny up. Poor Nanny, half asleep climbs out of bed, her gold crucifix, medals, scapulars and vest wrapped around her neck.

In her bare feet and nightdress, her bucket in hand, hobbling down the stairs. The bucket for peeing (the bathroom too far for her weak bladder) was emptied, rinsed, disinfected, and the gas turned on. 'You be careful and turn that gas off when you're finished.' She limps back up to bed. Ready or not, Esther and Nanny get their breakfast lathered in butter and salt, both of which Nanny loves but is strictly forbidden. Still, they both eat every morsel every time.

On the morning of my Holy Communion, a beautiful sunny day in May, I was awoken from my tired slumber by Esther and my mother running around our bedroom, Esther had stayed the night at our house. There they are unwrapping, patting, fluffing, flapping my beautiful snow-white clothes. I sit on the side of my bed and rub my face, bleary-eyed and gummy, my hair high, and magnificently set in a balcony of rollers. Yesterday I was brought to the hairdressers, a large front room in a Georgian house across the street. I had imagined that hairdressing salons were places of glamour, where grown-up ladies entered and re-appeared coiffed, manicured and radiantly beautiful.

The reality was quite different. The room was potent with perfumed lacquer and the smell of rancid lotions poisoned my nose. There, old ladies sat under dryers and read ancient magazines and stared at me, as I got nearly thirty rollers, what felt like, imbedded into my head. By the time I'd left the toxic place, my head ached. I complained to my mother that I felt bumps poking out between my rollers, but she told me it would be lovely tomorrow, and it didn't stop me talking.

My grandmother had bought me a shimmering gold medal, a white prayer book and, to my delight, a beautiful white lace bag with ribbon and frills delicately gathered around the opening. My slow awakening was somewhat disturbed by my mother and Esther embarking on a subdued but determined battle to dress me.

'Would you not put the hoop over her vest? There's no room for a slip.', directs Esther. 'I'm putting her slip on first, then the vest, then the hoop', insists my mother.

And so it went 'I'd sit that headdress back off her head a little bit and pull them curls down.'

'I like it forward, the curls will drop naturally, it's lovely the way it is.' I was a pawn in a tug of war. A contest my mother would naturally win.

'I just want to put my dress on. I'm sick of listening to yous', I begged them, bored of their fussing. 'Don't be cheeky', they both say together.

I wore a long dress, underskirt, hoop, sheer sleeves with long, elegant, gathered cuffs. A parasol, frilly socks, and a Tudor white headdress. Finished, I stood firmly on my pedestal.

All day I looked at my feet because for the first time in my young life I was wearing my very own pair of high heels. White leather with a strap, the two-inch tan leather block, placed me high, taller than I'd ever been. I loved high heels and would climb into Esther's cardboard box in the corner of the box room, to put on her boots and walk down the stairs. 'What are you doing up there? Don't come down them stairs. You'll be killed in them boots.' And before I can hobble down, she runs and lifts me; 'What did I tell you to do? You're very bold.'

My mother, father, brothers, sister, Esther and I, went to St. Andrew's Church, Westland Rowe, where, for the first time, I was to receive the body and blood of Christ. The ceremony was lost on my young soul. More interested was I in my new elevated position. My coveted job to bring the gifts to the alter went awry and was cut short when I clicked, pranced, slapped and tapped up the long aisle of the church in my new two-inch, white leather 'high heel' shoes. The people beside me giggled, as my teacher pulled the gifts from my hands, before my job was done, while hissing something into my ear. I felt my cheeks hot and red as she glowered at me for the rest of the ceremony.

The car rocked me to sleep as we zig-zagged across the mountains to see my aunts and uncles. They wait for my visit, cards in hand, lined with money. Thoughts of what I'd spend my money on had kept me awake for the previous three weeks.

'Your only gorgeous! A model for a coddle. Ah, she's beauriful. Where did you get her dress?' The tea, cakes, and sandwiches, like their kindness are never-ending.

Let That Be the End of It

I am now seven years old, and all grown up. Easter, my birthday, communion, and the Whit weekend have come and gone. The August bank holiday weekend has arrived, and my cousin, Sarah, is in my Nanny's house for the day. We both have new outfits as was my family's tradition. New outfits were bought for Christmas (two), Easter (two), the Whit weekend (1), August Bank Holiday (1) and christenings, birthdays, and parties.

Sarah and I decide to walk down to Timmy Murphy's shop to buy a yoyo each. It was also an excellent opportunity to show off our new Ra Ra dresses. As we stroll along chatting, Sarah freezes; 'There's Nelly, let's run.'

My first instinct is to cross the road and run, but I think about it and remember what Nanny said. Besides, I'm older now and understand more.

'It's ok Sarah, we're not going to run. We'll just walk by and say hello', I calmly say, my voice shaking. We both look straight ahead, and walk quickly, and are nearly passed Nelly when I get the courage up to say, 'Hiya Nelly.'

Well, with that, Nelly leaps from the front steps of her house and screeches at the top of her lungs, 'F******kkkkkk ooooooooff!' We run like the hammers of hell and scream ourselves hoarse with fright!

'Run, Sarah, run!', I scream. To my horror, Nelly is running behind us and screeching: 'You, f***in bitch ye I'll kill you.'

We run down the road, over the bridge and into Timmy Murphy's shop. By this stage, I am crying hysterically. Sarah is white as a sheet and shaking. We sob as we tell Eileen what had happened. Eileen walks outside to see if Nelly is there; 'She's not there; she's gone. Too cute to come in here. That's disgraceful.' It took her half an hour and two ice pops to calm us down.

We ran all the way home on the other side of the road and told our Nanny when we got back. We were both still shaking, and I was still crying, frightened and disgusted with myself, but mostly I was angry. Angry at myself for trying to be nice and angry at my Nanny for making me!

'I told you she was a bitch. You made me be nice to her! She said she was going to fuckin kill me! It's your fault!', enraged, I shout at my Nanny. I knew I wasn't allowed to curse but I thought under the circumstances I might just get away with it.

'Now, now! Stop dat! That's not nice', she wouldn't give me a pass. Not even on this occasion. I continued, 'Well I only said hello because you told me to. She tried to get us and chase us and was screaming. She ran out of her gate after us all the way to the bridge.' In the middle of my rant, Nanny wiped my face with a wet face cloth and barely moved her own. Her eyes glazed over. She was thinking ...

After what seemed like a very long time, she finally spoke, 'I'll see her meself.' That was it. Again, there was no shouting, no name calling, and no threats. Not that she ever did stoop to such low-brow antics, but given the situation, I thought she should at least try. She walked into her little kitchen, hands in her pinny and started talking to herself. She did this regularly, usually when something was on her mind. From my position on the couch in the living room, I could see her over the counter.

She was at the big pot, turning a rack of ribs with a long fork and in deep conversation. I tried to listen to what she was saying, but she was too far away. There wasn't another word about Nelly and for the rest of the evening she remained silent. Esther nodded in Nanny's direction and winked at me as Nanny ate her toffees and watched TV. We both knew she was different this time, and something was brewing.

Two days later Nanny arrived through the door laden down with bags of shopping. She kicked off her sandals, and as she sat in the chair, she let out a huge sigh of relief, 'Will you get me slippers me feetsh are killing me, hang up me scaaf there. I saw that Nelly one in the shop, well I got a hold of her. I ate her without salt! I told her, if you ever roar at any of them childerin again, you'll get more than apples off a me. Do you hear me?', says I to her. 'I'll break your effin face do you hear me? Now that's the end of it.' And so, it was. Nelly never again looked at us. We never looked at her, and Esther was warned to keep her mouth shut. My Nanny was a very gentle lady, but when she got angry, though it was very, very, rare, you better look out!

*   *   *

In my world, there already exists two older brothers, each child two years apart. I was now ready to join these two mavericks in action. They were the best fun and my best friends, though Esther was my very best friend. They could make camps out of bunk beds, ramps out of wood boards, buggies from old prams and bungie ropes from sheets. They generously included me in their many adventures. Although in hindsight I was probably the test pilot, as opposed to a respected member of the team.

Us children slept in the large 'front parlour' while our parents slept in the room next door, on the middle floor. Another family lived in the 'top rooms.' We shared the hall door. A year after my father returned from 'his trip' to San Francisco, my little sister was born. A sweet and gentle child who was 'not an ounce of trouble', according to my mother. Us four kids would soon be joined by my two younger brothers, to make us six.

In our bedroom there stood shared bunk beds for the boys, wedged against the wall to the left. My sister Carly and I shared another set of bunk beds on the right side of the large Georgian windows. A smaller bed was set along the opposite wall, where an upright piano lay slumped in the corner. The victim of many a 'Hooley', the piano had been played, bashed, and banged into a retired drunken submission. The carpet in our room was an ornately patterned, gloomy, deep green, the ceiling tall and centred by a grand antique chandelier.

Late one evening, my brothers were having such an excellent time jumping from the top bunk to the chandelier, and then landing on top of the piano, that I demanded to join in. The piano, which had been struggling for many years, was now giving way under the heroics of *Starsky & Hutch*. The last few jumps had caused the front left foot and rear right feet to buckle inward, so it was depressingly lopsided, not to mention deadly dangerous.

Blatantly ignoring their numerous rebuffs, 'You're too small, you won't be able to reach it, it's too high for you, you can't!', I climb up the ladder and nimbly and foolishly jump from the top bunk to the chandelier.

A lack of forward planning compounded by my inexperience prohibits my swinging from chandelier to piano top. I let go and crash to the ground, and at the same time, the piano's feet fold flat underneath, and it crashes back denting the wall. Stunned for a few seconds, I have no warning as a swift, but mild jolt lifts me off my feet. This, compounded with the thump of me missing my target and the fright of seeing my father standing over me, makes me cry. Everyone else in the room cleverly feigns sleep.

'I thought you were dead! Are you hurt?' My father is standing over me, his face ghostly white.

'No', I nod, getting into my bed.

'Are you sure?', he insists, rubbing my back and checking my face, as he wipes my tears. 'No, I simper.

He soon recovers his composure, knowing I'm not injured, 'Well get into that bed then! What were you doing? Look at the piano, you could have been killed! You won't be going out for a week! Get into that bed! If I hear another word from you ... ', he shouts as he leaves the room.

I get into bed and put my head under the covers, still shaking but giddy from my flight, though it was hard to sleep on a summer's evening. Especially when the thoughts of not going out for a week plagues my mind, not to mention not being able to spend my Communion money given to me by neighbours, family and friends. *Doll's World* and a thousand cola bottles would have to wait. The big old Georgian windows in the front 'parlour' allow the sound of children playing to torment my ears. It was some consolation that my father, in his haste, had forgotten to close the curtains. Back out of bed and standing at the window, the evening sun warms my face and the carpet beneath my feet, but also compounds my persecution. I can see my friends, red-nosed, freckled-faced, running free, squeezing the last drops of joy from the exhausted sun. I long to be out on the street.

His cowboy boots click on the lino, and the waft of *Old Spice* still fills the room when my father shouts, 'Go to sleep and be good for your mother, night in God bless.' The front door slams. His cowboy boots, denim shirts, a rhinestone belt, and worry beads, remnants of his time in California. He could carry it off, as he was confident, big, and strong. I admired him, and when he wasn't shouting, my father was high-spirited, lively, spontaneous, kind and the best of fun; 'Kids you're not going to school for a week. We're going blackberry picking to the country. I bought us a mobile home!'

Sometimes I'd get to stay up and watch him get ready to go out. He went out every night. After tea, my mother would iron his shirt and jeans, while my father took his bath. The fire piled high and roaring in the cosy, dark, beauty board covered kitchen. The tablecloth and dishes cleared away. Us kids washed and dressed for bed. The smell of steak and onions still loitering, mixing, mingling in the air with the swirling smoke from the chesty fire, that every now and then lets out a cough. I sit in my nightdress on the worn, brown, tweed couch while my mother plaits my hair, and I watch…Watch his wrist as it swirls the brush into a luscious lather. The razor gliding down his sloping jaw, clearing a path of snow-white fluffy cream. He hums a song as his hand pulls his jaw to the opposite side. The old, smoky mirror hanging by a black chain over the kitchen sink seems to blur his vision of himself. At thirty my father is handsome, hardworking, audacious, and smart, but he is not single …

'Daddy where are you going?', I ask. 'Out. Up to see your Nanny and Esther. I'll be home early', he looks at me, but is answering my mother, though she never asked a question. I knew his work was done, when he poured the red and white bottle upside down and slapped his face.

'Night be good for your mother, night', he says as he kisses my head good night. My mother doesn't look up.

Granda

We live both on the middle floor and in the basement of the tenement house with our adorable grandfather Tommy McQuillan, otherwise known as 'Macker.' My Granda, my mother's father, sleeps in the back room, behind the kitchen in the basement. A smoky, dusty room with cigarette butt filled ashtrays, coats over the bed all year round, various instruments in all stages of production and ancient furniture strewn with disintegrating books. 'Macker' likes to read.

He also plays the banjo, guitar, mandolin, ukulele and drinks Guinness to a band playing. His cigarettes of choice are '*Players* or *Woodbine*' or anything he can get his hands on. Browned fingers 'a pint' in hand, and plumes of smoke, 'Macker' is also an excellent storyteller.

He tells us children he worked 'the ships' around the world and starts most sentences with, 'When I was in the Congo, or was it Papua New Guinea?' He fills our heads with terrifying stories of his time with the head-hunters and cannibals of South America. Tribes, chiefs, sacrifice, and intrigue are his speciality. Though we learn later that he has never actually left Ireland, it doesn't matter. He weaves us a magical world of escapades, adventures, exploits, treasure and treachery, and we love him for it.

He's a mechanic and greases his hair with butter from the butter dish, leaving big black fingerprints in the butter. He drives our mother crazy.

'Look at the butter! Daddy!' She hurls the butter into the bin, dish and all. In a fit of temper, my mother can clear a counter or table full of dishes in two seconds flat....to the floor. She is unique, talented, brilliant, and definitely fiery!

Granda is a 'great mechanic' (according to my father) and also a competent engineer who has spent years delivering coal by horse and cart, and on the barges that weave through the canals around Ireland. His services are also regularly required by his friends and neighbours, and he is always willing and ready to oblige.

My mother's cousin, 'Smasher' regularly visits our house. He is a very nice, gently spoken man, an artist, a horse trainer in his early sixties, and a former heavy drinker, raiser of Caine and destroyer of pubs, hence the name 'Smasher.' He likes to recall the evening his ex-girlfriend's parents unveiled my grandfather's handy work to him.

'Well Bette' he told my mother 'You know I love your father. Well, wasn't I in Susan's house for the first time and your da came up in conversation? Well, when I told Susan's mother and father Macker was me uncle they were as happy as Larry and brought out the whiskey. You'd think he was King Farouk himself the way they carried on, lovely people, the best in the world they are. Well, they were thrilled with me and dying to show me the toilet Macker built for them.

'Come in, come in', says Susan's father as he pointed to the toilet in the middle of the room; 'Look what Macker did for us! There's a job. Isn't that beauriful!'

'Well,', said Smasher to my mother, 'I'm telling you,

there in the middle of the bathroom was a toilet built on a two-foot block. It was slanted, tilted to the side and you'd have needed a fuckin step ladder to get up and sit on it, but they thought it was the most beautiful toilet ever built.'

Smasher, unbeknownst to himself, was also caught in a web of intrigue, involving my grandfather and subject of an investigation launched by our family doctor.

The mystery as to the whereabouts of my grandfather's ever disappearing tablets was launched on a dark December morning. It all began one dank and gloomy morning when, having just finished our breakfast, our family doctor burst through our scullery door. So completely frustrated, angry and envious, was the doctor of my grandfather's complete lack of regard for both his own health and the doctor's advice. That he barely excused himself as he blew into the room.

'How are you Mrs?', he said to my mother, 'Well, I've been in next door with your father.'

By now, we were living next door to my grandfather, a few doors down from where we used to live in The Square.

'Your father had a black pan of sausages, rashers and pudding sizzling over the open fire. A cigarette in his mouth and a pint on the grate, the ash falling into the pan. And had the cheek to tell me to pull over a seat and join him!', said the doctor as he flopped down in the middle of our couch. The doctor went on, removing his scarf, gloves and overcoat; 'Says your father to me, "Let there be no panic amongst the troops, doctor. I had a think about it, and I realise what your problem is? It's traffic!", he told me "Traffic! You need a driver to drive you around, doctor", says he "and I have the man for you." He tells me his friend, Bill Steele, is a great driver and he ONLY wants a hundred pound a week for doing it!'

'Well Mrs', the doctor fumed, 'There's something wrong with this picture. I've had two heart attacks and a bypass, and I'm only sixty five! Your fathers in there and is eighty years of age, smoking thirty cigarettes a day, drinking like a bandit, and having a fry! And his 'friend', 'the driver' he's talking about is my patient. He's eightty, deaf in one ear and nearly fuckin blind! But the reason I'm in here today is that I'm giving him prescription after prescription for relaxers and sleeping tablets and he hasn't one left in there! And I have to find out what in the name of jaysus is he doing with them!' The doctor, exhausted by his temper, slumps back into the chair.

'Now doctor', calmly starts my mother; she could be hilarious, when she was acting at being serious; 'You don't be getting upset over him. There's no point. There's not a bother on my father, he smokes and drinks like a fish. Doesn't listen to a word you say or do a thing he's told. You stop worrying about him. He doesn't worry about anything. He doesn't have the worrying valve; he never did. That's why he's living so long.' She looks over at me, shaking her head, trying not to laugh, then carefully pours the boiling water into the teapot. She drops the tea bags into it one by one and stirs the steaming potion slowly.

'As for the tablets, I'll ask him about them myself. Now, you sit down there and don't be worrying. Will you have a cup of tea?'

'I will', he answers.

My mother's face remains perfectly serious while the doctor sits and drinks his tea, but the second she bids him goodbye and closes the door behind him, she collapses into tears of laughter. 'Every time I think of me da trying to organise Bill Steele to drive the doctor I go into hysterics', she laughs until tears fall down her face, barely able to tell me; 'He's doubled over with a stick, can barely cross the road and blind as an effin bat!'

The next morning my grandfather comes into our house for breakfast and is subsequently questioned about the mystery of the missing tablets.

'Don't mind that doctor', he tells my mother, 'He's an effin eejit'.

'But Daddy', she insists, 'Where are the tablets? What are you doing with them?'

'I take them every day, and I might a gave a few away. Poor oul Smasher was bad with his nerves for a while there. I gave him a few and Bill can't sleep, so I gave him a few. And I gave poor oul Jack in the shop a few sleepers after Marti, his cockapoo died. Sure, the poor fella was inconsolable. And sure, what harm? Doesn't Aileen throw me a few blue ones if I run out, and I her, and sure I take the rest. What is all the fuss about?', he asks my mother. There it was, straight from the horse's mouth, my grandfather, unbeknownst to himself, was the oldest drug pusher in town.

'Will I tell you what ails that doctor, will I?', my grandfather, in his infinite wisdom, asks my mother, 'I'll tell you! He's a bad-tempered, liverish oul goat. Always shaggin giving out. And if he keeps going on the way he is, he'll die young, like oul Rooney in the corner shop.

He died of bad temper! A bad temper can kill ya, did you know that?'

'Well Daddy, you just can't be giving away your tablets; they are on prescription. The doctor was very annoyed and said he won't be giving you any more if they keep disappearing. Do you hear me? He'll get into trouble.'

'Oh, I won't, I won't', he pets his friend, Duke, our loyal Alsatian, our house miracle, having survived parvo, distemper and an attempted coup by a wild cat and our delinquent budgie.

'All the same though, it's an awful shame he wouldn't let Bill drive him. We'd a made a right few bob outa dat. Have you a small one there please... with a bit a cake?'

My mother pours him a whiskey, cuts him a slice of cake for his breakfast, and chuckles to herself.

We weren't the only ones who thought our Granda was hilarious. Every Christmas, our relations call by on Christmas morning to have a pint with him and talk about 'years ago.' These tall, well-dressed, respectable friends and family file down our basement steps one by one to cheers another year with the most senior member of the family. They chat and laugh and remind him of the holidays he took them on with our grandmother, his kindness to them as children, of how much fun they had with him. I watch as my mother's cousin Joe recalls a story of my grandfather playing Halloween games with them. My grandfather put an apple in a basin of water with coins embedded into the apple. The children had to put their heads into the basin, then try to take a coin out of the apple with their mouths, as their hands were tied behind their backs.

Our uncle recounts this story to our grandfather and can't stop laughing; 'Tommy' he says; 'You used a basin that was more like a bath, and you'd have wanted to be a fuckin dolphin to get that coin out a da apple!' The party have tears running down their cheeks. They come to pay homage to the old man every year, without fail, and when they leave, he sits in front of the fire, rubbing the dog with tears in his eyes, happy, warm, loved.

A Wedding

Soul-searing wails wake me from my slumber. I stumble out of bed through the charcoal green moonlight shadows and onto the top of the stairs. Wiping the sleep from my eyes I see Esther lying at the bottom, her face buried in her hair, her arm covering her head, her body rising with each sob. She's muttering to herself. I can't understand what she's saying; I stand frozen and don't go to her. The sight of her helpless, slumped on the stairs, horrifies me. The glass streetlight glow warms her delicate, beautiful arms, her sobs turn to moans. Her long, elegant fingers point like a stunned ballerinas and pluck a lightning shriek from the depths of my being.

In an instant, my grandfather appears, snow-white vest, flannel pyjamas, his body wiry, worried, and leaning over her. Moving her hair from in front of her face, his own ashen and shrunken, 'What's wrong? What happened to you, what happened to you?', he begs her. 'Tell me, tell me!', holding her hair back, trying to turn her around. Her voice barely audible through moans, she whimpers; 'Daddy, Daddy, Daddy, what am I going to do? How will I go on?'

'What happened you? What happened you in the name of jaysus, what happened you?'

'Daddy, Daddy, he's getting married. He's getting married. What am I goin to do?'

'Come on, come on, hold on to me, you're ok, you're

ok', he says, her limbs so lank, he's barely able to carry her. 'She's ok, she's ok, come on, come on.' He gently puts her into the bottom bunk and me in at the end; 'She's grand now; you go asleep, good girl go to sleep.'

When he's gone, I crawl out of the end of the bed to check on her; 'Are you ok, Esther?', I whisper, 'I will mind you. I will mind you. Shush, go to sleep, shush.' Her soft hair smells of lemons as I rub her head. The big yellow moon lights her face, and the tear that falls onto the back of my hand I wipe it away. I can't remember falling asleep, but Nanny got me up for my breakfast when I was still tired.

Everyone is whispering, 'Is she alright? I can't believe it. The dirty bowsie! The dirty louser!' She's not good. She's not herself, not well at all.' Hushed conversations in worried rooms.

'Are you getting up to play with me, Esther?' I sneak up to the room and ask her.

'No, I'm not well. I'll talk to you later', she tells me from under the covers. 'Go on down to your Nanny.'

'I'm fed-up, Nanny.' I tell her, 'I've no one to play with.'

'She's not going to that wedding.' My Nanny slams the big pot onto the cooker. 'Go home if you want to, I'll ring your father; he can come up and collect you.' She snaps at me but is glaring at my Grandad, 'I'm telling you she's not going.'

'She wants to, he's her friend, we can't stop her', my granddad never wants to upset Esther.

'Over my dead body, I don't care who or what he is, she's not going. Is he trying to kill her! I say she's not

65

going and that's the end of it!' My Nanny is angry now.

'She knows him all her life', my aunt tells our neighbour Anne. 'They were always best friends and when they started going out with each other, sure we all thought that was it, they'll be getting married next.' I hear them as I sit playing on the stairs; 'I mean she knew he had a new girlfriend, but she didn't think it was serious. She thought they'd get back together. He was always mad about Esther; I mean always since as long as I can remember. That's why it's such a shock.'

'Is she still in bed?', Anne asks weeks later. 'Yes' my auntie Vera mutters wiping a tear from her eye.

Even when I'm home with my mother, she's Esther's best friend and confidant; she speaks of nothing else; 'She fell in the door here today sobbing. She's insisting on going to his wedding. I don't think it's a good idea. You'll have to do something' she pleads with my father.

'Do something, what can I do? Come on now, are you telling me he doesn't know what he's doing? He doesn't know how she feels about him. Of course he does! He's a grown man. He knows exactly how she feels about him. I told her stay away from him. I told her! A fuckin asshole he is, not a pot to piss in. Going around like he owns CIE. He's only a fuckin busman not a fuckin banker, fuckin asshole. Do you hear the accent on him, he's from around the corner, the oul one, his mother, is the very same, a fuckin consequence from a corporation house like meself. Social climbers, a fucking suit on, calling to me mothers? I asked him was he going to a funeral, cos he was dressed like an undertaker? She's after been told a hundred times! I told her. I said be careful. Watch him. He won't marry you, I told her! He hasn't the guts. Making a fuckin show of herself going to his wedding.

"He's me friend." Me friend, me arse! They were going out together, how can they be friends now?' My father slams his mug of tea down and storms off to work.

'He wants me to go with him in the wedding car', her head in her chest her mint green silk blouse soaked in tears that fall like rain. Today she doesn't even use a tissue, her silk sleeve wipes her running eyes, nose, and mouth. Her eyes cast down and barely open, her voice fades to a whisper. My mother makes the tea, her face frozen in horror, reflected in the kitchen window, her eyes on stalks, she swallows, and queries the source; 'Do you think that's a good idea? Are you able for that?'

Esther's heart is in her right hand. She doesn't have the will to answer. Overcome and desperate, I silently throw myself onto her lap, then hunker down to see her face under her hair. I put her hair behind her ears the way she does mine. I want to cry with her, for her, but I stop myself; my mother is here.

'You go on and play, good girl, she's ok' my mother tells me. The door is only closed behind me when a train of tears gush out of my left eye, a few more than from my right. I want to scream and tell Esther to stop! She wasn't the same anymore, and I want her back to the way she was, laughing, singing, dancing, games and picnics, all gone, stopped, eclipsed, night, night, all because of the stupid wedding. The whispers, the crying, the giving out, I want it all to stop and for us to return to normal, to Mr Forshaw's, to cleaning, to Meath Street. I even thought about including Nelly but couldn't bear it, so I changed my mind for wine gums and *Dallas* or *Dynasty* by the fire.

These days, even her body is lost, almost invisible in the corner chair.

'If you seen her, Maura', Esther tells my mother 'She's like the back of a bus! I'm not joking with you. She'd a woolly jumper on her, a pair a slacks, a pair a sandals me mother wouldn't wear. A big pair a thick glasses, she's the image of his own mother. Her hair swept to one side, a comb over and a beige fuckin trench coat, like *Columbo*.', finally, in the twilight-speckled front kitchen, I hear the two friends scream with laughter.

The Square

'Name this tune!', our stout elderly neighbour John saunters past in what seems like the same tweed suit since I can remember. Grey hair, red face, cream shirt, tweed waistcoat, trousers, and jacket. A snow-white cotton handkerchief tied in four corner knots on his crown, covering beads of sweat that roll down and soak his too-tight collar. 'Thank heaven for little girls. For little girls get bigger every day', he sings across the street in a perfect French accent. He's in his late seventies and still in great voice.

My father replies '*Gigi*, Maurice Chevalier!'

'Brilliant, brilliant', says John, 'You can't beat Hollywood! I'll sing another one before you go. I have often walked down this street before.....' My father finishes, 'But the pavements always stayed beneath my feet before, ... knowing I'm on the street where you live. Lerner and Lowe, John, *My Fair Lady* beauriful, great songwriters. They don't write songs like that anymore.'

'They sure don't, they sure don't, I'll see you later kid', John says in a perfect American accent as he slowly walks off, his gait wide, his hand on imaginary holsters, baking himself in the summer morning sun. May, his wife, is a frequent visitor to our home, my mother's best friend's mother, she's slight, cheery, kind and beautifully scatty. She runs by to mass, runs to town, runs to the shops, runs to the butchers, and sometimes stops for chats at the railings or has tea and cake on the steps.

In our 'Square', a large Georgian square, there was once a park, that is now a tarmacadamed playground. A large shed-like structure, in the centre of this playground facilitates activities, and stores equipment. In The Square we play basketball, round towers, skipping, tennis and football. Gated railings stand firmly on guard, surrounded by Georgian houses on three sides in various states of disrepair.

This exquisite June day is so hot that the tarmacadam sticks to our feet and scorches our soles. Even the chewing gum that I pick up and am not allowed eat, is easy to get off the ground. Little bodies of all shapes and sizes yelp, scream, and leap with delight, through a cascading, glistening waterfall of cool, spraying, crisp, clear, crystal water. Swimsuits, shorts, underwear, and vests are soaked in exalted galloping gushes courtesy of the caretaker, scourged into spraying us kids with a fire hose from the hydrant.

My mother calls me and is passing sandwiches covered in bread wrapper through the railings when my father drives into The Square with a striking silver trailer attached to his hatchback. In my child's mind its sole purpose is for all us children to play in.

'Can we get in Da? All of us?', I scream, 'Can we pleassssse?'

'All in, all in!', my father bellows, and nearly thirty of us children pile, trample and squash into his trailer as he does forty laps around our square. Screeching, singing, sticking our tongues out and signalling the poor unfortunates that missed the jaunt, we stop just in time as Mr Whippy pulls up. My father buys every one of us an ice-cream; generous to a fault, he never leaves a child out. From his poverty-stricken youth, he knew what it was like to be the child that stood by, watching.

Scooters, bikes, race cars, dolls, skateboards, skates, trains, prams dolls houses, and pool tables fill our house. Our parents buy us everything they didn't have growing up. If money is tight, we got second-hand. Presents come all year round and are scattered throughout our house. Nothing has a place, and so nothing can be found, much to my father's frustration. He is acutely organised and forensically clean.

Summer projects, singing, dancing, talent contests, birthday parties, day trips to Butlins and family holidays at our mobile home by the sea filled our inner-city summer life. Playing with our friends in the playground or getting the odd slap from another child was all part of daily life. Though sometimes, we were invaded by neighbouring clans from local 'flats' and ran home for our lives. For some reason, it was concluded amongst these children that our tenement houses were lavish palaces of Persian carpets and luxurious furnishings and that we were 'snobs.' I was caught …, by the hair and 'reefed' a couple of times. When questioned, as to what I had done to deserve such treatment, the offending invader's shameless response, 'Because you think you're great.' Flawed reasoning for a physical assault, I know, but the sentiment accurate enough.

Running into our kitchen for a diluted drink, I crash into my mother. She's pulled the twin tub into the middle of the room. Even with the window open, the stench of nappies, washing and washing powder is thick in the air. She wipes her shiny face with her hands; she's slight and exhausted. Her distraction allows me to escape up our back stairs out the open hall door and into Kathleen's next door. Her door was open all day, as were most doors in our square. Hers is the flat up the back-return stairs. I open her kitchen door overlooking the backyard and sit at her table, my feet barely tipping the ground. I'm a regular uninvited visitor.

'Hahaha, did you come to see me?', she laughs.

'Yes', I nod, transfixed by the picture hanging on the wall of a crying little girl with dark hair and big eyes.

'What are you looking at?', she asks as she throws her dry clothes on the kitchen table, having walked the three flights up the stairs from the backyard washing line.

'Is that you when you were a little girl, Kathleen?', I ask her, both disturbed and curious.

'It is', she sincerely tells me.

'Why were you crying', I ask her.

'Because I lost me Mammy, but I found her again', she tells me.

'Look what I have for you', she places the largest packet of orange chewy sweets I've ever seen on the table and a glass of orange cordial. I sit and I eat, and we chat while Kathleen puts on the evening dinner. I like her a lot.

'I've some lovely dresses for you, that are too small for Kathy, hold on and I'll get them for you', she returns like a gipsy princess with the loveliest pink, yellow and green dresses I had ever seen, with big skirts and short sleeves. Her husband opens the blue door; 'Hiya K', he gently kisses her on the cheek. 'What are you doing in here?', he asks me. 'If I see another child in here, I'll scream. What do you want?', he scrunches his face to make me laugh. 'Little bastards yous were out on bikes at seven this morning.' I smile and ignore him; nobody minds him, one day he roars out his window at us, other days he gives us sweets. I like him. We're always the first kids up and out on our street, to the annoyance of our neighbours.

'You can't talk; wait till Tommy gets his hands on your son', she tells him.

'What, what did he do now?', he asks her.

'He ran in this morning, ran down the back stairs and dived on the poor man in his bed. Tommy said he nearly gave him a stroke.'

'Poor oul Macker sure he has him the way he is. He ruined him, lets him away with murder, cos he makes him laugh.' It was true the impromptu paraglider was one of my grandfather's favourite kids; he, alongside my brothers, were the labour and resource team for the 'McQuillan Invention & Creation Bureau.'

A few months later, I told Kathleen that my auntie Esther had the same picture of her as a little girl, crying. 'She bought it in Spain.', I told her.

'Go way, did she? Imagine that me picture all the way away in Spain?' She was happy I told her ...

I later learned almost everyone in the country had a picture of the little girl with the crying eyes, and she wasn't Kathleen! Haha ...

I loved growing up in the inner city. The incessant city noises filled the electric air with excitement, drama, and ecstatic suspense. Noise of friends, all class of Dubliners, shouting, laughing, working, playing, singing, joking filled our days. The Square is a fascinating collection of nutcases. Every day in summer, someone is on their steps, tea biscuits, cakes, dinners, and ice pops are handed out freely. Front doors are open. Some of the houses are set in flats, some are lodging houses, all containing some of the most interesting and peculiar people, whose comings and goings are meticulously recorded by us children.

At nine sharp, Buzzer and Maggie True, two sisters who live together, march up the far side of The Square on different sides of the street. Sometimes, they outright ignore each other but get the same bus and share the same seat. Other days, they scream, insults, and trade blows as they scowl, jeer, and signal each other up the street to the bus stop. At 10.15 Mr and Mrs Maginelli, an elderly Italian couple in their late sixties, wheel a pram up and down the street with their over-fed black cat purring as they collect their days shopping.

On alternative days, Mrs Maginelli, stuffs a cushion up her dress and pretends to be pregnant. She frightens me with her craggy face and black teeth, but the adults around me talk to her every day like it's the most normal thing in the world. To add to my confusion, my mother tells me they are nice people and mean no harm. 'Bon Bon' goes for a whiskey at five every evening and comes home singing at eight. His white hair and beautifully coifed white moustache complement his chocolate hat and ancient suit. Haphazardly accessorised with a yellow shirt, polka-dot bow tie, blue handkerchief, and gold pocket watch, checked proudly at regular intervals on his journey. He delights at our frequent requests for the time and never refuses.

At 4.30 every day, Mr Wolfgang, a German professor who lives at the end of The Square, a rumoured worshipper of the occult and sacrificer of birds in his basement, clumps by. We are fascinated and afraid of him. So, most days, we march behind him, calling to him 'What time is it Mr Wolfe, one o'clock? What time is it Mr Wolfe, two o'clock? We continue up to ten as we take a step closer to him every time we ask. When we are at 10 o'clock and very close to him, having terrorised ourselves sufficiently, we run away, screaming. He never once acknowledges our presence.

Then there is the lady who breaks the jam jars out her backyard once a week. She walks past us every Saturday with a trolley full of glass jars clattering, clinking, tingling then that night smashes them with great gusto against her rented back wall. 'I'm sorry Mrs' she tells my mother one evening, 'For disturbing you, I'm not well with a broken heart. So, I go out and smash up the jars with me temper. My husband left me for my best friend.'

My mother tells her not to worry, she understands, but please to try to finish up early so as not to disturb the children.

I have friends of all ages and varied mobility. There is 'auntie Maysie', who I call on to sip tea, and devour freshly baked apple tarts. In her late sixties, a jean-wearing maverick, she sits with me on random afternoons and listens to my trials and tribulations as a budding actress. Every so often, she laughs out loud and cleans the inside of her ever-steaming glasses. I really like our chats and her too, and I always leave with gifts of old clothes and fabrics to add to my already extensive costume collection.

Peggy, the pharmacist, provides me with bags of

testers, lipsticks, pan sticks, eye shadows and liners for my frequent treading of boards, in the plays and talent competitions that speckle our community.

On days when we're bored, we tie string to an unsuspecting door knocker, hide in the bushes and scourge the poor unfortunates that live in the house. We also tag along to watch the bigger boys 'rob orchards' and throw the bitter fruit they give us away. We tie wallets to fishing line on summer evenings, hide in bushes, and wait for a dozy drunkard to walk by (the more belligerent, the better). The more annoyed they get, the more the wallet moves, the more we laugh.

Kathy is Kathleen's daughter and my best friend, according to her. She's two years older than my eight years, a foot taller and a lot bossier. She's generally very nice to me, like a benevolent dictator, gives me her cast offs, sweets, and sage advice. But when disobeyed, she's triggered like a banger on a Halloween night, throws tantrums, expels me from 'the gang', and sends me home crying to retrieve all dresses, presents, or loans previously given me.

On rainy days, Kathy and I visit 'Mum Harrison' but 'only two of us at a time.' These visits are directed and co-ordinated by Kathy; 'We're going to Mum Harrison's for a smoke, come on.' 'Mum' the frail boned, tiny, sweet old lady, sits under a shock of white curls, listening to our childhood stories. Triumphs and woes are embellished to make her laugh and share with us her gummy smile and loose cigarettes. Her chuckles cheer our freckled faces as we puff and choke on plumes of sooty smoke and pretend to be grown up. Toasted and red, in front of her old range as rainy autumn drops, drench, and drip down the wavey glassed paned squares of her rotting windows. These visits were heaven to us. But soon enough our smoking club is shut down when Kathleen finds a half-smoked Woodbine in Kathy's jacket pocket.

We were summoned to the steps and cross-examined by our mothers. It worked out fine though, as I blamed Kathy, and Kathy blamed poor old Mum. Neither mother said a word to the old lady, so we got off scot-free without a single father being told.

Sounds of 'hooleys' fill our square on many evenings, summer and winter. Friends, neighbours, and relations, sit around kitchen tables, sip *Guinness*, brandy, whiskey, and wine. crooners, singers, and wingers, accompany pianos, mandolins, harmonicas, guitars, banjos, and ukuleles. Traditional, pop, and standards are sung. Gossiping and laughing adults on steps provoke a tired head out of a worn window, that might temporarily quieten them down; 'Shush, the kids are asleep.'

A pickled drunkard might sing his way home and start a howling dog's chorus.

The night stillness is regularly disturbed by Sunny, our drunken neighbour, and his nightly calls for 'Patch' his dog, who's five years dead; 'Get in you basterdin dog, where in da fuck are you?'

'He's dead Sunny, Patch is dead! You're wakin up the whole square!', a tired neighbour informs him.

'Wha? Well, fuck him anyway, and you too for that matter! In future, mind your own business. That's the problem with this square, yis are all nosy bastards!' Sunny closes his door.

Charm Bracelet

'Can I have your charm bracelet when you die?', I ask Esther, holding it up to the light, the back of the tortoise casts a sensational rainbow surprise through a diamond prism on the white wall.

'May God forgive you, the cheek of you! I'm only a young one.' She's sitting up now in the bed, in her crisp-cotton lemon nightdress, her pretty, lopsided curls, coiled like snakes on her head.

'Huh' I tell her, 'A young one' as I place the 18ct chunky charm bracelet on my arm, the weight of the gold trinkets pulls my tiny wrist downward.

An amber globe, a wishing well, an old pound note, a ballerina, a sports car, a horseshoe, a horse and carriage, a boot, a ruby globe, a tortoise, a wedding band, an engagement ring and eternity ring bunched together, a church, a five pound note, a bottle of wine, a love heart locket.

'There's a bride and groom, too- see when it opens? Can I wear it now?', I ask, knowing the answer.

'Me good bracelet!', she laughs. 'Put it back, You've some neck!'

I giggle, 'Well, can I have some of your perfume. I love that smell?', I ask but don't wait for an answer and spray it half a dozen times anyway.

'Stopppppp! Me good perfume! Wait until I get up to ye!', she laughs and pulls back the covers as I make a run for it and leap down the stairs.

'Get up. Come on, let's go to town! You promised me we'd get in early', I call back to her.

At ten years old, I'm now as tall as Esther. She cooks us a fry. Crispy sausages sizzling with the crunchy fat from the rashers, white pudding crispy and soft, black pudding thick and crusty, with tomatoes. The fat from the fry cooks the eggs and the fried bread. The black iron pan, too heavy for me to lift, is thrown between the four gas hobs. Salt is scattered where necessary, and sweet tea with milk is served on the side. Mouth-watering, salty and spicy deliciousness. I don't speak for a half hour.

'Do you like that? That nice? Will I run the shower and warm it up for you?', she asks, sipping her tea, enjoying watching me as I soak the salty buttery fried bread in what's left of the egg. 'I saw a lovely white trouser suit with a box jacket for you, for Easter. Will we go in and look at it?'

'Yes, but I think I want a dress', I tell her nonchalantly, too full to move. The yellow shower in the corner has a shower curtain that does absolutely nothing to stop the floor from being flooded every time anyone has a shower. The drain in the room, I'm sure, only for show, barely takes a drop of water.

'You're after flooding the place. Go up and dry your hair. Anne's outside.' She gets the tin bucket and mop to soak up the excess water and washes my feet too.

'Hay ye chicken', says Anne. She is sitting in the front room with a tissue in hand, her blonde bob sleek, her eyes pretty and blue, her lips pink and her left cheek purple.

'Heya Anne', I tell her passing through. Anne lives on the road, is Esther's friend and is always very nice to me. They are obviously talking grown-up stuff, and I am clearly not wanted. Half an hour has passed since I blow-dried my hair. The minute I hear the front door close behind her, I run down the stairs and casually ask Esther, 'What happened to Anne?'

'Nothing. I can't tell you', Esther informs me.

'You can't tell me?', I demand.

'What do you mean? You tell me everything. You CAN tell me. Tell me! Please, I won't tell anyone, I promise. I promise, please?', I beg her.

'No ... no ... I can't, I can't.' She ponders as she drags the hoover across the wooden floor.

'Please, please, I promise I won't say a word to anyone, tell me please', I implore her.

'Well,' she says, abandoning the hoover to the middle of the room and sitting back in her chair, 'She's after getting into terrible trouble.'

She stalls momentarily, head to the side, hand raised, 'Shushh', she says, 'I thought I heard someone coming in.' She liked to do this for dramatic effect, knowing full well I was dying to hear a story.

'Anyway, Harry caught her with her fella. There's murder going on. The other fella was the best man at her wedding. Wasn't she out a few months ago and didn't she meet him again after years? He was working the door of a nightclub; they've been meeting ever since.'

'How did Harry catch her?', I whisper, excited by the intrigue.

'Well, wasn't she out with her fella in the Wexford Inn, kissing him at the bar, when Harry's sister walked in and caught them? The sister told Harry, you can't blame the girl, that's her brother after all, but in anyway there was murder.'

'Oh, and why doesn't she just leave Harry then?', I ask, seeing no reason why this was a complicated story to begin with.

'She can't. What about the children, the house? It's not that simple. Harry said he wouldn't leave the house, or the children, and she can't leave her kids', Esther explains between long sighs.

'She knew when she was getting married, she didn't love Harry. She knew she was marrying the wrong man.' Esther stares into the empty grate, her eyes somewhere in the distance. She is lost. I know the sadness that sweeps over her is not far off. The subject is so dangerously close to 'You know who', I try to steer it away, lest our morning plans are delayed by tears.

'I think you're right', I say, 'I think I'll get the trouser suit with the box jacket', I inform her, standing up, having tied my laces. But I was too late.

'You know I went to his wedding, ... Daniel's wedding!', she says.

'No', I say.

'It was one of the hardest days of my life, that and burying me Daddy', she continues. 'I thought I'd die of the pain,' her head bowed, her thumbnail in her mouth.

I didn't remember much about my granddad's passing; I went back to Nanny's house for summer holidays and was told he was gone to heaven. I was rooting in his pockets 'in the wardrobe in da wall' when I found a moth ball and ate it. I thought it was a 'golf ball' chewing gum, Esther gave out to me and I'd to spit it up.

'I've something else to tell you. Anne said she saw him in Rathmines yesterday, she said he looked well. He was askin for me ... When I think of it, I should never have gone to his wedding, but I had to.'

'Oh?', I say, walking to the kitchen. 'Did she? I didn't know you went to his wedding', I try to shake the mood, act disinterested and bang a press to distract her. But I did know, I knew everything. My mother had told me all about 'You know who'; 'I never liked him', she said. 'He was a consequence, a jumped-up snob that wasn't fit to wipe her boots. But she loved him; he was her childhood best friend. She couldn't help it ... '

My mind floats back to her lying on the stairs that awful night, my stomach drops, and I feel a lump in my throat. I remember the weeks and months that followed, the empty house, that trip to the hospital. The white corridors, the people in wheelchairs, walking, talking and moaning, frightened me. I only went once. Esther was sitting up in a bed, she cried when she saw me and hugged me so tight I couldn't breathe. I sat in the bed with her and begged her to come home; we both cried. Then Nanny said we had to go. Nanny wouldn't take me again, but I knew when she was going to see Esther because she brought her nightdress and underwear, sweets and Lucozade. I bang the press once more to stun myself out of this memory.

'Are we going to the graveyard tomorrow?', I ask her, trying to divert the subject once again. This time, I was successful; the maintenance of my grandfather's grave, in that moment, more important to her, than the topic of her badly broken heart.

'Your uncle Brian's coming in the morning to go over

with us. When Esther said, 'go over', she meant it, literally. You see, my grandfather's grave was across the road from my grandmother's house. Well, across the road, through the neighbour's garden and over their back wall. Just behind that wall was my grandfather's grave, facing the house he spent his life in. I always thought it was very considerate of him to die and be buried across the road from us. A ladder from the backyard and there we were, over the fifteen-foot wall and standing at the grave.

'Knock into Mary and tell her we're going over to the grave', she tells Brian, her younger brother. Lucky for us Mary's side entrance was always open but for a small steel gate, whose bolt occasionally jammed. Skilful and brave Brian sat on top of the wall, allowing us to climb to the summit one by one. When stationed at the top he pulled the ladder over and lowered it down to the other side. 'Me nerves are gone, hold me now, I'm warning you', Esther says, commencing the intrepid climb up the steel steps.

'Come on. I have you, don't be stupid', he tells her, 'Hold on to me back.'

As she throws her leg over the wall to sit at the top, she slightly wobbles and grabs Brien's back and at the same time, lets out a savage scream, 'Oh Jesus, Mary and Joseph!'

'Will you stop outa that!', Brian scolds her. 'Sure, if you fell, I'd pick you up, wouldn't I', he winks at me and laughs.

'Stop effing messing you I'm warning you', she shouts. Another 'Oh Mammy' a few steps more, and she's down the other side. Standing at the grave, a plastic bag is thrown down with a suddy cloth and fresh flowers.

'Name a the Father, Son, Holy Spirit Amen. Bless yourself' she tells me.

The following bleak March Monday morning the mood is sombre as myself and my father enter my grandmother's house. Nanny is sitting in Esther's chair, wearing her 'selling pinny' and wringing her hands.

'What's wrong with you mother? The smell a that fuckin bleach! Put on that radio, the place is like a fuckin morgue', my father says as he playfully rubs my Nanny's shoulder.

'What's wrong with you Lilly? Did you lose the few bob in the bingo last night?', he's boisterous and joking. But his face darkens when Esther looks away.

'What's wrong with you, mother?', he asks again, startled.

'Me Mammy has to retire. She's after been up with Dr Mc Rally getting her results.' Her heart's not great and he said that's the end of her pushing her pram', Esther relays the message while Nanny looks at the ground nodding.

'What am I going to do without me few bob?', Nanny asks herself out loud.

'First of all, that Mc Rally fella is a fuckin quack. Secondly, what test was this you had and with who?', my father demands, taking off his brown leather jacket.

'They tested the valves in me heart, and said if I don't stop, I'll have a heart attack. It was in James's Street hospital; the heart specialist did the tests.' Mc Rally is after telling me to get rid of the pram that I have to stop selling. I won't have a shilling. What about me customers, me friends... they depend on me?', she asks. Her disappointment and heartbreak palpable but swallowed like almost every hardship in her life. So bewildered was she at the prospect of losing; not just her livelihood, but her identity, her social life, her way of life. That when in the following days, she repeated her story, she could barely say the word 'friends' without gulping down her tears. She never drank or smoked; talking to people, all kinds of people, was her therapy, her pleasure, her love, her life.

My father tries to lighten the mood; 'Don't be worrying about the few bob. I'll look after you, mother. Have you ever wanted for anything? I'll be looking after you, the two of you, don't worry about that. He kept his promise. He'd been looking after her all his life and gave her his first wage packet when he was ten years old. Since the age of seven, he'd gotten up at 5am every morning and went with her to the market, to collect her stock. At thirteen years old he found a wallet stuffed full of money and handed it in. The gentleman who owned it, a prosperous builder, gave him a coveted 'trade' as a painter. At twenty one, he owned his own company, and she never wanted again.

'Mother', he tells her, 'You'll have to listen to the doctors this time. Your poor legs are fucked anyway, and sure don't you deserve a rest. Working all your life, it's about time now you enjoy yourself! Put your feet up.'

She nodded her head impatiently, dismissing his notions of enjoying herself, 'Would you go long outa dat, what would I be doing at seventy three years of age retiring? Enjoying meself? Sure, I do enjoy meself, doing me work, meeting me friends.' Her protestations were pointless. It was decided by all of her concerned thirteen children, she'd have to retire, give up selling. She was getting on, her 'pinny' was to be hung up, her pram parked.

For seven long weeks, she walked out her front door first thing every morning for 10 o'clock mass. Head in the air wrapped in a headscarf, she never looked left nor right, while her pride and joy, her loyal friend, her old faithful, sat under a bush in the garden, a bread board a top. Shivering, dejected in the freezing March rain, shaking, and squeaking in the stormy April showers. Cut off, ignored, not mentioned. Severed like a gangrened limb, like a lifelong friend that through one hapless transgression was sent to the furthest Siberia, ostracised, shunned, discarded, avoided. Things were all quiet on the western front until one early May morning, my father took a detour on the way to visit my grandmother's house. It was my birthday and her and Esther had presents waiting for me. My father, unusually quiet, meandered through the back streets of Smithfield, over the bridge and crawled up Christchurch Hill, the steepest in the city. All seemed normal until he swerved suddenly to the right-hand side of the road. And there, like a rambling child escaped from an unlocked garden, was my Nanny, a fully loaded pram of fish and selected vegetables, talking to herself, pushing her pram with all her might, up the hill.

'I knew it! I knew it' he screamed, 'I fuckin knew she was up to something; she was too quiet! Not a word out of her yesterday! Plotting and scheming! I knew it!', as he rolled down the window, he shouted at her.

'What were you told? Out selling again after what the doctor told you. I knew you were going selling. I knew it!', with that he pulls the handbrake and jumps out of the car.

I hear him tell her, as he helps her up the hill, that she's an awful woman who won't listen to what she's being told. A woman who refuses to see sense and how she'll know all about it if she drops dead. She walks in front of him as he struggles, sweating bullets, pushing the pram up the hill. Her head in the air, strolling ahead, waving her hands by her side, shushing and shooing him; 'Mind your own business and stop making a show of me. I'm old enough in the tooth to mind me own self. Go long outa dat!'

He gets back in the car breathless, exasperated, exhausted and as he pulls away, he curtly waves and shouts at her, 'You don't be out long! I'll leave a few bob at the house for you. You're an awful woman!'

And as we slowly drive around the corner into Thomas Street and stop at the traffic lights his exasperation slowly changes, and a look of sheer pride and unwavering love appears across his face. Just beside us is Nanny again, smiling, happy, her 'pinny' on, her gold earrings glistening in the sun; 'Look at her', he says, 'As strong as an ox. All her life out doing that. She's some fuckin woman.'

New Kid In Town

'Bless yourself, there's a beushiful story', my Nanny says, tears in her eyes. It was after 11 o'clock at night and The Late Late Show was just over, and it was about the miracles of Medjugorje in Bosnia. The sick, depressed, crippled, and maimed were being cured, reborn, delivered. I blessed myself to please her, but I didn't believe a word of it. I mean, how could it be I thought to myself, you went there you prayed, and you were cured?

'God bless us in the name a the Father, the Son and the Holy Spirit, bless yourself. Wasn't that beushiful?', she asks me.

'OH YEAH NANNY IT WAS WONDERFUL!', I tell her, but she tutted and gave me a look.

Tap, tap, tap, there's a faint rattle on the window. Esther calls, 'It's me Mammy, I forgot my key.'

Nanny opens the door. Esther rushes in and runs to the bathroom, then comes back and slaps the arm of the armchair at the side of the fire.

'It was a great night up there tonight. The band were brilliant, Phil (Philomena) came down with Martin and his brother. We'd laugh ... they were brilliant.'

'Were Willie and Matt there?', Nanny asks her.

'Yeah' Esther looks down at her feet ... 'They were grand, they were ok.'

'Wait till I get me hands on them. They were in here earlier and the Willy fella was blind drunk at 8 o'clock in the evenin. I made them sandwiches; a cup of tea and I told him to go home to his wife and childerin. He said he was going straight home and you're telling me the two of them went up there to that Club together? I'll see him in the mournin and the other fella's not much better. And when I went to the press, there was lumps gone out a tomorrow's ham, the two of them ateing it with their dirty hands! I'm going up now. I had me supper and a cup of tea. You get one there and ate a sandwich before you go up. Don't turnin on that grill. Nightsh! I'm ashamed of me life of yis, drinking, disgraceful!' Nanny says giving her a withering look from toe to head.

Esther's blue eyes pop and stare as she puts her finger to her mouth to shush me.

We wait in silence until we hear Nanny clump up to the top of the stairs, her bucket in hand, and bag full of prayers, a creek tells us she's closed her door.

'Hold on, I've something to tell you,' Esther says as she makes her way into the kitchen, putting on the kettle and toast under the grill. 'Do you want a slice a toast? She's like a demon tonight, they must have really annoyed her. She'll give it to them tomorrow, that's for sure. Anyway, weren't we all up there tonight, your auntie Phil, Martin, me, Mary and Bridie and wasn't Martin's brother Paddy over from England. He's only gorgeous, real dark like a gypsy, black eyes, only beautiful. Well, didn't he ask me up to dance to Joe Dolan, *Good Looking Woman*, well he swung me around the floor. We'd a great night. He told me I looked gorgeous. He said he loved me hair, me blue eyes!' With that she twirled me around the room and we both sing every word; '*When God created a woman for me, he must have been in a beautiful mood. Oh me oh my you make me sigh, you're such a good lookin woman.'*

She loses her balance; we both fly onto the couch, then slide off it onto the floor, kicking the coal house door with a bang.

'Shush she'll kill us', she giggles.

Thump, thump, thump; 'What are yis doin down there!', Nanny shouts.

'Nothing ma, she fell, she's grand ... He asked me could he walk me home and I said no, no thanks. I said, "I'll walk meself, thanks." He was pleading with me, begging me, but I said no. Hold the bone and the dog will follow, isn't that right. He said he'd be at the party tomorrow night, so you'll get to see him. He's only gorgeous like Omar Sharif', she laughs, gulps her tea and takes three giant bites out of the buttery toast.

'Oh God ... I feel sick. I can't eat anymore; come on let's go up.'

'Don't forget you have to bolt the front door', I tell her as I climb the stairs. That night I smile as I lie in bed looking at the stars, Esther is happy again ...

'Have you anything to eat?', my auntie Phil asks Esther as she rifles the kitchen press the next morning; 'I'm dying with a hangover; we didn't leave until after two, I'm starvin. Paddy was mad about you last night, wasn't he? He's a great job in London, Esther.'

'Do you want a cheese, ham and tomato sandwich with a packet of crisps? Batch or pan?' Esthers impatient and 'Not in the mood today to run after any of them!'

'Oh, batch loaf, loads a butter!', Phil says.

'PLEASE!', Esther eyeballs her.

'Please,' Phil says in an overly sweet voice as she winks at me and makes a face; 'Have you a loan a twenty for tonight?'

'No! I've no money, don't ask me,' Esther snaps.

'Ah please. We have to go out tonight to the party with Paddy and Martin doesn't get paid till Friday. Please we'll give it back to you; you know we will, please?', Phil begs her.

'I'm warning you', Esther tells her; don't have me to ask for it. I want this back on Friday, do you hear me? Not Saturday, not Sunday, not Monday, Friday! Just come up here Friday and hand me that money, do you hear me? Esther puts the twenty pounds into her hand; 'Did you give Mary the tenner towards Vera's present yet?'

'I'm giving it to her Friday. Thanks, you're very good.' Phil says putting the twenty in her bra.

'You better!', warns Esther

'Do you like him?', she asks Esther.

'He's all right,' Esther tells her, giving her a huge sandwich with crisps on the side.

'Well, he's mad about you. Oh thanks, that's gorgeous, are they *Tayto* or *King* crisps?', she asks Esther, devouring half the sandwich, with one bite.

'Excuse me, what did you say *Tayto* or *King*? Do you want me to take them back?' Esther grabs the plate: 'Get yourself demolished and your arse polished!'

'I'm only messin with you, stop, it's gorgeous, ahhhh!', Phil screams a laugh and grabs the plate back; 'He's a nice fella, isn't he? I think he's gorgeous looking, a model for a coddle he'll do for a stew!', Phil laughs her head off and wipes the tomato from her T-shirt.

Esther, wily, remains non-committal.

'What time is it? Oh, Jesus, I better go, Martin'll have a search party out for me. Right, I'll see you later, I'll see you up there, we'll be there about half seven. Thanks!' Phil leaves in the whirlwind she came in.

'I thought she'd never go. I'm jumping into the shower. Are you all right there?', Esther says, then turns on the telly; 'There, you watch Worzel; you love him. I've your pink dress ready for tonight; they'll be all ragin when they see you! I won't be a minute. Don't answer that door to anyone.'

*   *   *

'Who has the best legs, me or her?', my auntie Phil asks me at the party that night.

'You!', I tell her, not only because she has the best legs, but because, besides Esther, she's the funniest, wildest and kindest of all my aunts.

'Good girdle yourself,' she tells me, then sticks her tongue out at my aunts; 'See I told yis, even the child knows it! What are you goin to sing, Esther?'

'*Your Good Girl's Gonna Go Bad*, Tammy Wynette', Esther says.

'They're playing your song Phil!' a well-intentioned passer by tells her.

'It's not her song, IT'S MINE!', Esther says as the band play the intro and call out her name. She runs to the front of the stage and holds up her arms, two of the band members pull her up on to the stage, she's in fits of giggles as she takes the mike.

With the red-light glow behind her, she belts out her

favourite song like she's a singer in Vegas. In her mini dress, knee high boots, and big hair, she's the most beautiful woman in the room. Phil is swinging me around the dance floor and we're singing as loud as Esther. I know the words to every song she loves because she plays them repeatedly.

This was a family party, my auntie Vera's thirtieth birthday party, to be exact. There are at least two hundred people there and most of them are up dancing. I am the youngest cousin present, but to my bitter disappointment, I am only allowed to stay until 10 o'clock. Disco lights bounce around the floor, and I'm smothered in hugs and kisses, as cousins, aunts and uncles greet me. A huge buffet lines one of the walls. Curry, chicken, chips, salads, sandwiches, cakes, you name it, they have it. A seven-piece band provides the entertainment. At first, 'They play a few numbers to get the place warmed up', according to Esther, then later invite the guests up to sing. Every single one of my father's family can sing and not just in a corner at a party, on stage with a mic, and a band. Everyone has their own song, too. To sing someone else's song in the company, whether a family member or friend, is considered a great transgression, a terrible flaw in one's character, sacrilege.

'Can I go to the bar for you, Esther, please?', I beg.

'Get me a Macardi and coke, bring me change back, don't lose that money!', she tells me. Her tipple of choice used to be Brandy, but now it's the exotic 'Macardi' and coke. The jaded barman tells me it's '*BACARDI.*'

'Did anyone say you were nice? Did anyone like your dress?', Esther asks me.

'Isn't her dress gorgeous on her, isn't she gorgeous?', she threatens the company.

'Ah massive, your gorgeous, a little beauty, my auntie Vera,' tells me, 'Give us a twirrille.'

'They're calling you up, Bridie go on they're calling your name to sing!', Phil shouts.

All blonde and gorgeous at six feet, my auntie Bridie walks up to the steps of the stage, takes the mic and sings her song, *These Boots Are Made for Walking*, actions and smiles were included; excellent job, round of applause, done.

The next person is called up on stage, she leans over and tells the MC what she's going to sing. The first eight bars of Phil's song *Nobody* is played. Eyebrows are raised, looks are exchanged, sisters, brothers, cousins, neighbours and friends, comment, scowl, and glare. 'That's our Phil's song' someone says. 'She knows quite well it's Phil's song,' Esther tells the table, confused. Phil is at another table with my uncle Martin, grinning like a Cheshire cat.

'Nothing, say nothing,' Mary says, her hands waving in the air.

'That's not right, that's not nice, who invited her anyway' Esther tells my auntie Mary.

My auntie Mary gives her a wink; 'I'll tell you later, members can bring guests.' It seems the brazen robber of songs was an old colleague of Phil's. Who it turned out, was trying to get Phil sacked, because Phil was getting her friend to clock her in to work on time, on the days she was late, bringing her father-in-law to the hospital. This brazen robber, who Phil, only the week before, may or may not have tripped up in the bingo when she was running up to collect the spot prize ... was obviously still a bit sore ...

'Would you like to dance, Esther?', the dark-haired stranger asked her.

'I would, thanks, Paddy' she said.

This was a 'slow set', and they were dancing to '*Islands in the Stream*'. When I was leaving with my Daddy, I ran and gave her a hug and a kiss goodbye. She barely noticed I was leaving.

* * *

September meant back to school. I haven't visited Nanny's house in weeks. Esther's always with her new boyfriend, Paddy. I'm disgusted with her, if she's not with him she's talking about him! Halloween, my favourite time of year, has come and gone. I dressed up as a witch. Antoinette O'Brien said, I was one. I told her, so was her ma. Evenings in our Square are chilly, wet and dark, but it doesn't stop us from staying out on the street for as long as we possibly can. The smog in the air is thick, as is the smell of briquettes, logs and coal. Chimneys puff out dark grey plumes of smoke as the heavy sky leans on my head. Our fire is lit every morning and kept stacked throughout the day; that and the bottle gas fire in the kitchen and an electric fire in our bedroom are our sources of heat in the old house.

We fight over who stands in front of the gas fire, and my poor sister burns her leg. We toast bread on it, too, but only when the babysitter, Tina, is minding us. She's fourteen, the best babysitter ever, and lives 'out the back passage', yes through the hallway downstairs, out the backdoor and through the yard, is her house. Just last week, she was babysitting when she saw a mouse in our kitchen, jumped on the table and cried until our parents came home. We laughed. She scrubs and cleans the kitchen, brings us sweets, and gives out to our Grandad all the time: 'Tommy, I'm only after cleaning the place, and now you're ruining it before they come home; I'm telling them on you!' Carly was always her favourite child. Years ago, she was inconsolable because Carly didn't win the *Bonny Baby Competition* in the community hall. 'She should a won it, I had her gorgeous, they weren't as nice as her', tears flow down her cheeks.

'It's ok, don't be crying', my mother consoles her; 'Bring them into Roches Stores and get them ice cream; she did that anyway, almost every day.'

Years later, Tina came again to help my mother in the house but left after just one week. My two younger brothers, 'them little bastards', refused to move their bodies, or feet, or do what they were told when she was cleaning and 'Were cheeking her up to the eyeballs!'

'They're too spoiled, and I wouldn't deal with them! Ah no, I couldn't put up with them, I'll have to resign,' she tells my mother eating a breakfast roll and sipping her tea. The breakfast roll got on the 'slate' from our friend who owned the breakfast shop around the corner; 'Can I pay you Friday for them, Marie?', I ask her every week.

'No problem. Take what you like there.' Marie's a class act.

'Anyway, Bette', Tina continues, 'it's your fault, sure

you have them ruined, they won't pick up a thing after themselves. You'd need to go to a therapist to try and stay sane in this house, I do me best to manage the madness in me own head, and you're in the thick of it here with them boys. Well, I can't put up with it!!!' Our weary friend continues. My mother nods in agreement; 'You're right, I couldn't agree with you more', she says.

Tina looks at my mother, 'Jasus, Mary and Joseph, I don't know who's madder, them or you!', they roar laughing.

A Proposal

His proposal is nothing special, I conclude. I'm on the stairs 'earwigging.'

'Will you come to England with me, Esther?', Paddy says.

'And do what?', she snaps. 'Live with you somewhere?'

'God no ... Esther, will you marry me?', he asks her.

'I'll look after you, I've a great job you'll want for nothing I've a lovely place there. I love you Esther, I want you to be my wife, to have a family with you', he says

'Oh ok. It's very quick isn't it, I mean we don't know each other that long ... Yeh well ok, well I'll have to tell me Mammy, and they'll all have to come over. I'm not getting married in England ... I wish me Daddy was here ... Yes! Yes, I'll marry you! Get up off the floor, you'll ruin your leather trousers!' They're laughing ...

'Esther, You've made me the happiest man in the world; look at me I'm shaking. I knew the minute I saw you I wanted to marry you!', he says: 'Do you like it? They're not the biggest diamonds in the world but I thought it was dainty and pretty ... like you.'

'I LOVE it, it's beautiful, I can't believe it ... Sit there. I'll make you a cup of tea. I can't wait to see the rest of them. Me Mammy's asleep ... I'll tell her when she gets up.'

I run into my Nanny's room and shake her in the bed; 'Esther's getting married, Esther's getting married.'

'Wha, wha, whatsh, stop it, stop it, wha, whatsh?', she's tired today; only her eyes move.

'They're going to have a baby and get married', I whisper to her.

'Who, who is', she stares at me, trying to understand what I'm saying.

'Esther and Paddy' I heard them, they're going to get married.

She throws the blankets off the bed; 'What were you told about earwigging, it's not nice. Did he ask her to marry him ... what she say?'

'I told you Nanny already, yes, she said yes! And they're going to have a baby he said.'

'In the name of Jesus, Mary, and Joseph isn't this shockin', she mutters; 'Sacred Heart of Jesus, help me.' She's nodding her head now.

'When they get married', I tell her.

'When they get married, they're having a baby? Not now?', she asks.

'They're going to have a family he said, when they get married, he said. I told you Nanny! It's NOT my fault Nanny! I'm going down!', I storm out of the room, sick of her questions and moaning.

'Come back', she laughs 'come back.'

'No!', I tell her.

'Are you getting married?', I ask Esther as I enter the room.

'I am, look at me ring, d'you like it?' She gives me a hug and shows me the three small, but pretty diamonds on the gold ring.

'I'm going to England; will you miss me? I'll have

me own little girl like you, but you don't worry you'll be coming to stay with me, and you'll still be the apple of me eye.' I didn't say too much because Paddy was there, and Nanny was coming down the stairs, but my heart sank a little bit when she said she'd have a little girl like me.

'I'll be happy he's a nice fella; he's very nice to me, he cares about me. He's mad about me and he's not afraid ... He loves me for me.' I didn't want to hurt her feelings, but it was a silly thing to say, of course he loved her for her, who wouldn't. He was the lucky one as far as I was concerned, and I was the loser; as the days went by, my excitement turned to gloom. Soon, I would be losing my best friend and the most precious person in my life.

'Is it far?', I ask her: 'What bus do I get to you?'

'Bus to where?', she asks me, confused.

'To England, what bus do I get to you?', I have to repeat myself.

'Oooohhhh, in England, ah, you get the ferry first, then the bus to me, ohh emm, the forty-four' she says finally.

'Is it far away?', I ask her.

'No not at all, twenty minutes on the bus.'

'The same as Meath Street?'

'Exactly the same as Meath Street', she answers, then hugs me tightly 'I love you, you're the apple of me eye.'

'I know'. I tell her 'I will miss you', I want to be happy, but when I think of her leaving me, I just want to sit on the ground and cry until I'm sitting in a puddle of tears.

'Stop, I'm not going for AGES, and you'll see me every week. What'll we watch? *Dynasty,* wait an we see what *Alexis* is wearing tonight, her clothes are always gorgeous!'

We snuggle on the couch until I fall asleep, which I usually do.

Although my spirits are crushed at the thought of her leaving me, I can't lie, I'm quite intrigued at the prospect of going to England. I imagine my Nanny and me, getting the ferry then the bus, every Saturday; and oh, what an adventure it will be. Everyone's talking about it; Paddy lives in a place called Brixton, and there are loads of Irish and Jamaicans living there. I'm not sure what a Jamaican is, but somebody said they were all black, and Paddy said they're all lovely; he works with them.

It's Friday evening and Nanny is blowing her nose and dabbing her eyes on the couch.

'What's wrong with you Nanny, are you not going to the bingo?'

'Esther, she'll be going to England soon; I'll miss her', she tells me.

'Don't worry Nanny', I say, 'We can get the forty-four bus to her when we get to England. We can go every Saturday, Esther says so.'

'The fouty four is itsh?', my Nanny laughs, 'every Saturday she said.'

'Yes Nanny, see we'll see her every week.' She chuckles to herself, and I'm glad to see her smile again.

'Getsh me me sandals, I might go down the bingo when she gets back. Do you want to come? Bridie's bringing Sarah.'

'Oh yes Nanny!', I tell her, 'We might be lucky and win the jackpot!'

She laughs again; 'We might! It's a rollover, a thousand pound!'

The weeks went by and plans for Esther to move away were in full swing. Paddy came over and back from England to see her. It was agreed between Esther and me, on several occasions, that I was still the 'Apple of her eye, her number one, her best friend in the whole world', and would remain so even if she had her own child.

'Who was the chap on the bus? How do you know him?', Paddy asks Esther as he closes the door.

'He's an old friend from years ago', her voice trails off.

'We met Daniel on the bus; he was asking for you Mammy,' Esther tells my Nanny.

'Was he?', my Nanny says sharply. 'Sure, we haven't seen him in a long time, is he still married?', she asks Esther.

'I don't know, I didn't ask him' Esther tells my Nanny in an 'impertnint' manner.

'There's sausages and pudding in the pan there for yis ar tea. Is there an umbrella there in that coalhouse, look in there, it's lashing out?', she says.

'Here Nanny', I climb in and give her an umbrella.

'Is me good walking shoes in there too, pass them out to me, it's too wet for me sandals.', she says, and I do.

'Nightsh and God Bless' she says, drowning herself and the rest of us in the holy water from the holy water font at the front door.

'Why aren't the birds going to bed, they're still singing?', I whisper to Esther later that night.

'Because it's springtime, that's why and they're happy and excited to be alive,' Esther says.

'I know but it's very late, they should have gone to bed already, I'm tired an I don't want you to go to England' I tell her.

'I'm not going to England. Go to sleep, good girl', she says with a yawn.

'She's not going to England cos she doesn't love him, and she doesn't like his leather trousers ... They're not for her.' Esther told me not to say anything about the leather trousers or about her not going to England, but I was so happy, I forgot and blurted it out to the company, which consists of my aunts, Vera, Mary, Bridie, Phil, Francis, Anne, Esther, Nanny and me.

Esther stands with her back to the fire; 'I'm staying here; I'm not going to England.' she announces and gives me a stern look.

'What? What? Are you for fuckin serious?' Phil shakes her head in disbelief; 'What about Paddy did you tell him? Does he know?', Phil asks her.

'I told him yesterday, I don't love him, there's no point', Esther says, standing up with a cloth in her hand, pretending to wipe down the television.

'Are you sure, he's a lovely fella. Would you not give it a try, you might like England. Why are you not going? What happened? Why are you not going?', Bridie starts.

'Because I don't want to! That's why!' Esther is raging now; her nostrils flare, her hair looks on fire as she stands in the light of the window, her hands wedged on her hips.

'Brixton's great Esther, I think you're mad, to do what, sit here for the rest of your life! You might never get this chance again.' My auntie Vera is annoyed.

'Who said I'll be sitting here for the rest of me life?', Esther challenges her.

'I don't mean it like that, he's a lovely fella, he might

make you happy? Would you not even try it?', Vera pleads with her.

'She's right!', the oldest of them all, Francis, interjects; 'you were very bad for a few years, and I've never seen you so happy, I mean I hope you're not doing it for any other reason, I hope you realise this is a chance for you to be happy, to do something with your life. He's a gentleman and he wants to marry you!'

'Excuse me', Esther is raging now; 'who gave you the white fucking coat! The cheek of you, am I supposed to be thrilled that he wants to marry me! I don't love him; I'm not marrying him and I'm not goin to England!' She stomps into the kitchen and bangs the big silver kettle off the steel cooker bars. 'Do yis want tea or not!', she shouts across the room.

'She doesn't mean any harm, Esther I mean she's just saying, why would you stay here? He might make you happy. He loves you. I think you're mad, staying here for what? You could be in England having a ball. He's a gentleman. I don't want tea,' Phil puts on her coat.

'I hope you don't regret it. I really do. I'll see you tonight at the bingo, Mammy. I'm goin.' She marches out and slams the door.

'And how do YOU know?' My auntie Francis turns her attention to me; 'Cos you were earwigging, were you?'

The rest of my aunts tell her to leave me alone, make 'shush' noises and push their fingers to their mouths while Esther makes the sandwiches.

Nanny dozes on the couch, as they finish their tea and leave one by one. The sun dapples the coffee table through the net curtains, and the ticking of the clock is the only sound in the room. Esther puts an overcoat over my Nanny.

'Do you want to go down to Meath Street on the bus, put your coat on.' Esther whispers softly; 'Mammy we won't be long; we're just going down to Meath Street to get a cake. We won't be long.'

'Ok' my Nanny says, pulling the coat around her shoulders; she's snoring now. Esther nods at her, then smiles at me as we shut the door.

'Is she yours?', the lady on the bus asks Esther.

'Yes', she tells a bare-faced lie, 'that'll ill teach her to mind her own business', she giggles.

'Aw she's gorgeous; the image of you', the stranger replies.

This happens all the time ...

To The Country

'I'm going to wear my new yellow swimsuit. Mam said she'll buy us a lilo.' Carly tells me.

'Me Da said he's going to stay a week! I'm going to ask Mam can we bring Sheelagh?' Sheelagh is my mother's sister's daughter and another of my favourite cousins.

The day finally arrives, a beautiful summer morning in June and we are going on our summer holidays.

The open doored Hatchback with the trailer attached, sits on our street, ready to be overloaded with gas cylinders, blankets, food, toys, bikes, and kids.

It is 1984, I'm 11 years old and Ireland is in the grip of economic recession, but us kids are oblivious. Charles J Haughey, the Taoiseach of Ireland or (CJ to his pals) tells the Irish people to 'tighten their belts', while he buys his shirts in Paris.

Whatever my father can buy, that 'fell off the back of a lorry' or not, we have it. Cases of *Squeeze* orange juice, boxes of *Kellogg's Fun Packs*, trays of beans, bags of potatoes and wraps of meat, are all stuffed into the boot of our car. As he puts the last of his fishing rods into the trailer, he turns to see a boy standing in a sparkling white t-shirt, sky-blue shorts, a towel rolled under his arm, staring at him.

'Where are you going?', my father asks him.

'Nowhere, Mr Hamilton', the boy answers and looks at the ground.

'And you?', my father asks my brother's other friend,

who's also standing with his towel under his arm, wearing a yellow T-shirt and jeans.

'I'm going swimming to the canal, Mr Hamilton,' he says.

My father nods at their answers and then, without a word, goes back and forth into the house until he finally retrieves the last of his load, a pile of pillows, he throws into the boot, 'Were yis ever in Kilmuckridge?', he asks the boys.

'No, no Mr Hamilton', they answer together. He continues to arrange the boot while they stand there, nervous but not moving.

'Well do yis want to go to Kilmuckridge or not! It's all the same to me. It's up to yourselves, if yis want to go, come on ... ' he says jokingly.

'Aw yeh, aw yeh, Mr Hamilton, thanks yeh. Thanks, Mr Hamilton! Can I go home and tell me ma?', says the boy with the sky-blue shorts, skipping on the spot.

'Can I go home and tell my ma? Will you wait ten minutes on us?', shouts the other as they run off up the street at the speed of light.

'Tell her two weeks, yis pair a kennatts! And hurry up, don't be long, get back here quick,' he shouts after them.

'Aw thanks Da!', my brothers look at each other, grinning. 'But where will we all fit?', my older brother asks.

'In the trailer, where else, put down the duvets, pillows and sleeping blankets; I'll put the potatoes in the back to weigh yis down.'

'Aw thanks Da, thanks Da!', my brothers laugh, then push each other. It was a set up and my father knew it, but he couldn't disappoint the two boys.

'I want no messing out of yis, do yis hear me? Yis better get them tents out the back. Yis are gonna need them', he says laughing. 'I hope to jaysus it doesn't rain!' He settles the four boys into the trailer, packing them tightly with pillows, duvets, and blankets. 'I'm serious now, no messing. I'll take it very handy. Hold on to the side rails, wave if there's a problem, I'll be looking at yis all the way.'

'All right, everyone in here we go!', all squashed into the car and trailer, mother, father, six children and two friends. We excitedly commence our adventure.

I feel the sun on my face through the rear glass at the back of the Hatchback, behind the seats, a berth, a pillow under my head and miles of country roads rocking me gently. Mountains of purple, green, yellow, moss, hedges dotted with buttercups, roses, wildflowers, and a million multi-coloured bells ringing their scent and beauty in the hazy summer lush. I can see the four boys in the trailer lying in their fluffy mess, kicking each other, squinting, laughing.

Halfway to the country we stop in a glorious little restaurant for the toilet, burgers, chips, desserts, and ice creams.

'Sit down and shut up' at times, our arguing gets on my father's nerves. If you see him reach between the seats to swipe someone, you get out of the way. But mostly, this journey goes without incident, and we sing to the radio all the way there. Everyone is designated a song; 'Aw, here's your mother's song, *Run Around Sue*', he says, as she nods her head. 'Aw, here's your song, She (he calls me that for short), *Something Stupid* ', he roars a laugh.

'Shush Da, that's not my song…' I tell him.

The minute we arrive at our site, we jump out of the car, run into the mobile home, grab our bathing suits, towels, and run to the beach.

The walk from our site to the beach is my favourite. I walk in my bare feet to feel the heat of the tarmacadam sand sprinkled road; the sun roasts my shoulders, the smell of fresh lemon-scented grass mixed with the warm, sweet lavender-perfumed flowers and the salt air from the sea is ecstasy to my tipsy senses.

On my way, I pass country cottages with whitewashed walls, thatched roofs, little gates, parched drooped pink and purple flowers and barking dogs. Just before the beach, buckets, spades, lilos, and balls hang like candy from a tree outside the little shop with the wasp graveyard window. The smell of chips with salt and vinegar wafts through the air as I pass. Life is perfect, as pictures of every kind of ice cream fill my head and soon my mouth. Scorched on the sand I splash my way into the water. *Soda Stream*, crisp sandwiches, and chips, with a sprinkle of sand for lunch.

'Fish n chips' for 'tea', sausages, beans, bread and butter. After tea, my mother pours Calamine lotion onto our red skin and patrols the bathroom while we get ready for the local disco. Bang, bang, bang; 'Get out of that bathroom; you're in there an hour, everyone else has to get ready!', she tells Carly.

This morning, I open the small window on the top bunk to see pearls of morning dew glisten and sparkle on the lime and yellow grass, the warm air blows the smell of lemon butter and sea. The creek behind us trickles and swishes in my ear. My mother and her sister Mary are cooking breakfast, there's straw in my hair and kids in the tent. My mother's other sister Monique and cousins sometimes join us for a week or two.

During the week, my father returns to work in Dublin but comes back down to us for the weekend.

'Daddy's coming down today', I tell Carly, 'I'm going to ask him to bring us to the village; there's a toy shop there.' I love the hustle and bustle of his grand return.

'Who wants to go to the beach? Who wants money for the amusements? Empty your pockets. How much have you got? The truth!', he jokes and hands us all money. We are rich!

'Here's twenty pounds; go up and get fish n chips and burgers for the whole lot of us!', he tells the boys.

My mother is trying to figure out the constellations in the navy night star-sprayed sky. She stands outside the door, her head up to heaven; 'Is it Leo or Pegasus, Mary? Imagine we're hurtling through space right now; do you ever think of it?', she asks my aunt.

'I do in me eye. Though I'm not sure if it's Orion or is that in winter? Sure, shag it anyway. I'm going inside to listen to Cole Porter', she laughs. Tonight, we play cards, *Draughts, Snakes and Ladders* and snow. Just before the end of the card game, my mother jumps up and throws all the cards into the air. 'Let's play snow' she howls laughing. Luke, 'the baby', he's almost four, storms off in a huff. We think she's hilarious, but tonight my heart is truly broken because tonight is the last night of our holiday.

The next morning, my father is eating his breakfast, ready to hit the road. 'I want to get on the road before the traffic starts; if we leave it too late, we'll get caught in Gorey at lunchtime.'

'Can we go to the beach for one more swim please, Mam please?', we beg her.

'Ask your father', she tells us, too busy to look up from the pile of breakfast dishes she's washing in a basin.

'Go down now and be back by half ten, do yis hear me? I'm warning yis, now don't have me to come down for yis, go on.' In the gorgeous summer morning sun, we splash and swim like it was the last time in our lives that we would ever be in the sea.

Our departure is made all the more miserable when my father blurts out, 'Weather forecast said it's going to be a scorcher this week. Are you sure you don't want to stay another week?', he looks at my mother.

'No', she glares at him.

* * *

Sitting in the steaming classroom trying to figure out the percentage of the partially eaten orange for the sour-faced teacher, I long for those sunny days. So confused am I by the maths I'm failing to decipher, and this unseasonal September heat, I even think I hear my father's loud voice down the corridor. The click of his cowboy boots, the jingle of his keys on his jeans ...

'Thank you, this one, is it sister?', he shouts knocking on the door but doesn't wait for it to be answered and like a mirage he is suddenly standing before me.

'How are you doing? I need to get Sheila; we're going away for a few days. I was talking to the sister there it's all sorted', my father tells the teacher. I grab my bag and coat and run to him to grab his hand lest it's all a dream.

The dumbstruck teacher mutter's something about sister Mary Rose and glares at me as I leave.

'Are we really going away, Dad?', I ask excitedly as I run, trailing him through the school hall.

'We're going to the country, the weather's gorgeous for September, it's too nice for yis to be in school, and we can pick blackberries. Your Nanny and Esther are coming too, they haven't been on holiday all year. Your mother will make yis blackberry jam and tarts', he says smiling, rubbing his hands.

'Oh, Da, are we? Oh, great Da! Did sister Mary Rose say anything?', I ask, worried she might be coming after us.

'Don't mind that oul one. What harm is it a week off school. I'm your father. I know What's best for yis, where's Carly's classroom? What does she know?', he replies.

'Nothing,' I tell him. He laughs. When we get home my mother has almost everything ready and thrown into black bags in the middle of the kitchen floor.

The sweet smell of blackberries fills the air as we pick their blooming thorny bushes; bursting bombs of sweet purple juices tickle our tongues and blacken our hands and faces, eating as we fill our buckets. Bees congregate and feast on the overripe banquets. Delicious local honey glistens in shop windows. Bountiful are the plump, purple, sweet, blackberry, pretty puddings and jams that line the counter of 'the caravan' this beautiful roasting September morning.

'You're a beautiful baker', my Nanny tells my mother,

sitting in her flowery blue nightdress, eating apple and blackberry tart for her breakfast. 'Aw thanks Nanny', my mother says, 'I won three baking competitions at school.'

Out of the blue, a murderous roar comes from the bedroom: 'Ahhhhhhh, ahhhhhh, ahhhhhh get off me yis bastards. Yis are nearly after given me a stroke.' My teenage brothers, in hysterics, run by us and jump out into the field. 'We're after jumping through the skylight on auntie Esther.'

'They're nearly after giving me a fuckin heart attack, it's not a bit funny. Wait till I get me hands on them, ah that's not right!' My mother tries not to laugh but fails miserably: 'I'm sorry for laughing. I'll have a word with them; they're very bold. Sit down. Do you want a cup of tea?'

'You reared fuckin animals Betty. That's all I have to tell you. You reared bears to fuckin ate yeh!', Esther tells my mother. The room erupts. I love it when we have company.

The next summer, I am twelve years old, and it was just our mother and us on our holidays. As long as she can stick being on her own with us, we stay. My father used to stay longer, but these days he goes back to Dublin the same day. He was supposed to come last weekend but couldn't make it and this weekend too but didn't show up. We're still waiting on him ...

I saw Mam wipe a tear from her eye this morning, I think she's lonely, but she never lets on. Yesterday, I had to bring my younger brother Luke with us to the beach, which I hated. I didn't want to mind him, but sometimes I had to; I was building a trench, then turned around and he was gone. I panicked, and ran all the way back to the site, crying hysterically; Luke was sitting there with my mother, eating a bag of crisps.

I screamed at him, 'Where have you been, you know you're not supposed to leave me or the beach.'

'Leave him alone,' my mother says with a wink. 'Bertie found him way down the road and asked where he was going and he said, 'Home to Dublin. I miss my Dad.'

We laugh, - but out of the mouth of babes ... Being the youngest in the family, Luke was spoiled, indulged and hilarious. At four years old, on his first day at school, my father dropped him into his classroom, in his smart uniform at the local Catholic school for boys and said goodbye. My mother and father were about to have lunch, when there was a knock on the open window. Luke was standing there, and they ran to the door. 'I didn't like it, I'm not going back,' he said and walked right past them.

I missed my Dad too. I missed the fun of him arriving, buying us everything, taking us to the beach, and jostling with us. He was loud, and he was fun, but he could be volatile and bad-tempered, when under pressure. He was under a lot of pressure these days, more than we knew.

We'd moved from our rooms in The Square shortly after my tenth birthday. My parents were doing well with the company they'd started. My mother typed into the night to get the jobs and contracts, and managed the books, while my father organised the work.

Our beautiful new house with the huge garden, high hedges, five bedrooms, Tudor style interiors and French furniture, paled in comparison to our bedraggled rooms in the worn old house. I missed our neighbours and friends and the way things used to be. This new house was bigger but lonelier. My father's 'business' took him away more often.

'We're moving back to The Square, my mother tells us one winter's evening. My parents had bought two houses side by side in The Square; we were moving into one, and my Grandad was to live in the other. We were elated. My mother packed a van the next day, as was her style, with twenty full black sacks, two lamps, a box of knick-knacks, and this time, left my father for good. Though us kids still saw him every day.

Tears, Tantrums & Theatrics

I run into our basement, panic stricken, and call to my mother, 'I want to go to see *Dirty Dancing* Mam. Can I have a fiver please everyone's waiting outside; it starts at three?'

She nods yes, looks in her bag, purse, the utensil drawer, then her coat in the passage. 'Ah, look what I found?', amazingly she's almost always lucky and finds money; when she isn't one of us gets through our granddad's window. He used to live with us in the old tenement, but now lives next door; we're forever getting through the window. 'Granda, Granda, quick, we need money for the school bus! Now Granda! The bus is coming in five minutes!'

'Get a fiver outa me top pocket. Tell your mother I need it back on Friday', he never gets it, and he never asks.

'Daddy, I owe you money. I'll give it to you Friday', she tells him.

'You will not', he replies, 'Sure don't you give me plenty' and so she did; all of his life she cared for him.

A big girl now with my own friends in our Square, I spend less and less time with Esther and Nanny. My stays with them become less frequent, more taxing and the subject of fraught negotiations. A visit could turn into a summit.

'Do you want to stay?', Esther asks me, 'You can stay today if you like.'

'No, I'm going to ...', I try to explain.

'Ah why don't you stay. Stay with them, I'll collect you tomorrow and go up to the shop and get you a few sweets?', my father says to me.

'No, Da I can't. I'm going off with me friends to see a film later...'

'Sure, you can see a film any day, ah go on, stay', he insists.

'Aw leave her, she's going out with her friends, you might stay Friday, will you?', Esther asks me.

'Yes', I tell her 'I'll stay Friday', I don't want to hurt her feelings.

'And we'll go into Meath Street Saturday morning?', she says.

'Yes, great', I say, frantic to leave.

'Aw well, alright then stay with them Friday so, right come on then. I'll see yis later, say goodbye to your Nanny', he says annoyed, but resigned.

'Bye, bye Nanny, I think she's asleep', I tell him, relieved to make it out the door.

It wasn't that I didn't love them anymore or that they had changed from being adoring and wonderful to me, they hadn't. It was just that they now cramped my new grown-up style. I wanted to be free, an emancipated street urchin running on The Square with my friends, playing round towers and tennis, going on day trips and outings, entering dance competitions and talent shows, and doing all the things an outgoing twelve-year-old girl does. My father's bribes, my tears, my mother's diplomacy all in full swing; my battle sometimes lost, my defeat bitter.

'I don't want to go and stay with them tonight', I

desperately tell my mother. 'And besides, you need me here', I tell her. My mother's once vibrant health has long disappeared, and she's tired all the time and often sick.

Her health is tenuous, and no one can tell her why. Not the eight specialists or the doctor that attends her, sometimes twice a week. It wasn't just the strain of raising her six children almost alone; it was the mystery illness, the exhaustion.

'I'm bringing you up to your Nanny's later. They want you to stay. You said you'd stay with them today', my father tells me. 'They miss you. They're lonely.'

'She doesn't want to', my mother says, her hand on her hip.

'Why?', he shouts 'She already told them she was. She can't do that, they're waiting on her. She's going up', he glares at me.

'She can't', my mother's voice calm, her chin pointed towards the sky. This whole conversation like so many, is held as my mother stands in our basement garden looking up to my father, who is outside the gate on the street. 'She got the lead part in the play in drama school (a lie, a part, but not the lead) and has rehearsals in the morning. She can't miss it, or she'll lose the part; it's on in The Royal College of Music.'

He looks at me, and I catch on quickly; 'The rehearsal is in the morning. I don't know what time it's finished at. We have the space for the whole day, so we are going to run the play.'

'Well, you better ring them; they'll be very upset you're letting them down badly; you suit yourself, that's not fucking nice', he scowls.

'But I have to go, or they'll give away me part, it's not my fault', I plead with him.

'That's fucking terrible, you better ring them', he grimaces, nods his head at us and leaves.

But all is not lost, Nanny gets two buses down to my mother's house every Tuesday evening. One from Crumlin to town, and one from town to Pearse Street. So, I see her most every week and take her to the bus stop when it's time for her to go home. There, I wait with her until a bus comes to collect the precious cargo, while my mother stands at the hall door, waving, summer and winter until Nanny gets on the bus, they adore each other. Esther also visits and periodically helps my mother around the house, but she says we are too untidy for a cleaner, and 'Not fit to have a bin'. So she threw it out. 'What kind of people don't line the bin with a black plastic bag, and don't give the floors a good scrub every morning? You have to make them do it Betty', she lectures my mother.

'I know, I tell them all the time', my mother says.

*   *   *

'I want to be an actress when I grow up', I tell my mother at twelve years of age 'and I want to go to drama school. I called them today, they're on Georges Street, it's £95 for ten weeks, I'll ask me Da for the money when I see him.' I loved drama school despite the many remarks about my 'Dublin accent', the D4 accented Camerons, Fintons, and Allegras had to make way for an inner-city, working-class Dubliner.

The very first production I was in, that year at drama

school, was 'Ernie's Incredible Hallucinations'. I played Ernie's mother. Our opening night was in the National College of Music, Westland Row. It was midsummer. I was looking out of the window of the college when my family arrived. They piled out of a red *Hiace* van, all seven of them, dressed up and excited and beautiful; like travellers going to a wedding.

My mother said I was the best actress she'd ever seen. The night went brilliantly, and I won my school's drama award. Because of this early success, my mother was convinced I was on my way to a life as a famous actress, easily obtained with talent like mine! I was in full agreement! Around this time, I was in my first year at secondary school when I opted to take accountancy as one of my extra subjects. I despised it, and the teacher despised me. I told my mother of my conundrum, and she immediately went about rectifying it, when she walked into my accountancy class a few days later and addressed my teacher.

'Sheila won't be doing accountancy anymore; she doesn't like it', she told the red-faced, red-haired, wiry spitfire.

'But she has to, she picked it, it's her subject!', the riled teacher told her.

'No, she won't, there's no point. You see, she's an artist, a brilliant actress and a creative being. You're wasting your time and only annoying yourself; What's the point in that? She's better off in the library reading a book or drawing a picture. There really is no point putting a square peg in a round hole.' So that, as they say, was that.

As well as my mother, Nanny and Esther, my older

friend Celia is also one of my biggest fans. In her late sixties, tall, skinny with dyed, light brown hair set in curls, she wears red lipstick and is striking like a 1940's movie star. She is stick thin with long skinny legs, wears fitted coats, always with a belt, and mid-length skirts with thick tan tights. She has an old black Raleigh bike that she cycles everywhere. Every Thursday, she brings my mother and I, five autobiographies/biographies of Hollywood stars from the nineteen forties and fifties from Pearse Street Library. Greta Garbo, Lana Turner, Ava Gardner, Bette Davis, Joan Crawford, Ray Milland, Clarke Gable, Spencer Tracey and on and on, she's an avid reader ...

'Did you like that book? What did you think a poor Lana Turner, wasn't your man a bastard? What did you think of Joan Crawford wasn't she an awful bitch? Her and Bette Davis hated each other!'

Celia was a brilliant actress herself and often acted out scenes from famous movies. She was hilarious, and she knew it.

'Do you know what Bette Davis said about Joan Crawford?' Celia's head is cocked, her hand on her hip and her big red lips gleaming in a half smile. 'When I get that bitch, I'm gonna rip every blade of hair out of her moustache', she says in a perfect accent, then roars laughing. She stands at the bottom of our steps on summer evenings with me, my mother, and Celia's cousin, Maureen. We drink tea, tell stories, and laugh until the summer light slips from the sky.

'What's it all about? What is it all about? Why are we here?', she regularly asks one and all. She isn't just being funny; she really means it. She really is asking these questions seriously; she thinks about it and often. She has reason to; she'd suffered. Her first love died in a car accident; they were engaged.

Then, a few years later, she got married and had her only son. Her young husband died of cancer, leaving her alone again; she nursed him for the last two years of his life. She's extremely smart, way ahead of her time, and to say she is beautifully eccentric is an understatement.

Celia and her cousin Maureen, also in her sixties, are very close. Maureen is also a beautiful woman both inside and out, she had a sad story to tell. She was also married at a young age, to a handsome architect and lived in his family home, in plush Haddington Road. That was until her young husband fell from a scaffolding and broke his neck the day of their second wedding anniversary. Maureen was in the height of grief when his family turned her out of the house. She had to move back in with her mother into a rat-infested rented tenement room, until the city housed them. Maureen, a beautifully dressed, dignified, intelligent lady, was a lifelong friend to my mother and our whole family.

Celia and Maureen are hilarious together; they are as close as sisters and bicker like them. Maureen is very refined and likes to speak 'properly' and enunciate her words precisely. This annoys Celia no end. Celia has a thoroughly natural and beautiful Dublin accent. 'What are you talking like that for Maureen? Why don't you talk ordinary and stop putting on an act?'

To which Maureen replies in an even grander voice, 'What do you mean, Celia, I have always spoken like this?'

'You were born the same place as me Maureen and I

don't talk like that! You're only acting it' Celia says closing her eyes and turning her face to the evening sun.

Then, to send Celia completely over the edge, Maureen does not respond, but when Celia asks her another question, she points to her own lips and says 'Shusssh, I'm not allowed speak am I?' This kind of thing goes on regularly and only ceases when one of them bursts out laughing; you see they love each other.

Celia often gives me clothes for my stomping of the boards, as a young wanna be actress;

'Celia please can I have a loan of your fur coat, and a costume for the play I'm doing?', I ask her.

'Call around to the flat tomorrow at six sharp. Don't be late or you won't get in, do you hear me?', she says.

'I won't be late I promise!'

The next day I call around to her flat, I'm over an hour and a half late, 'Hey Celia, it's me, Sheila. I'm here to collect the clothes for me play.' She opens her letter box; 'No not today, you're late. I'm not in the mood for you today. I told you not to be late.' This is Celia at her very best, that's why I love her. She says and does exactly what she wants. If you are the doctor, the priest, the coal man or a friend, you get the same treatment.

'Ok, I'll call back tomorrow', I shout back through the letter box.

When I return the next day, she has the table set with cream cakes and a pot of tea.

'There's an *Irish Mist* for you (my age irrelevant), and on the way out, take the fox fur coat and the blouses you wanted.'

This was also Celia. They rarely make them like her

anymore. She was just herself, smart, funny, unique, and my friend ...

*   *   *

'Will we have a party, Margret?', my mother asks me. By now I'm in my late teens, 'Margret' is a name she calls me when she's joking with me; 'Come on, we need a party, life is too dull without one. Will you ask Lee to play the piano?'

'Oh yes, that's a great idea! I'll ask him to play, and we'll invite everyone, and I'll do the food and clean the house.'

'And I'll do the flower arranging,' my mother says; 'That's my forte.'

'That's good of you, Elizabeth', I tell her as I poke her arm.

I'd met Lee from Birmingham, Alabama, when I walked up the rickety stairs to Walton's School of Music and walked into the dull, musty, music room that overlooked the George's Street Arcade on the opposite side of the road. An upright piano, that had seen a war or two lay slouched in the corner, sheet music piled high atop. Then in walked Lee, a spectacular, coloured shirt, red jean-wearing 'gorgeous homosexual with curly hair' according to himself, with a handlebar moustache.

Pianos tinkled in the air, voices high and muffled sang the scales. I was wearing an old leopard skin faux fur coat and my sheet music from *Funny Girl*, like me, was a bit wilted.

Was I in the right place? I didn't really care; I was desperate for someone to save my artistic soul. I had trained as an actress, and now I wanted to sing, but I didn't know if I could.

'So, what do you want to sing?', he purred. I hand him my sheet music.

'Oh, I think I know this one!', he says. His slow southern drawl, with popping blue eyes campily expressing every word he sings. Pounding the keys, he begins to belt out, *'Don't tell me not to sit and putter! Life's candy and the sun's a ball of butter! Don't bring around a cloud to rain on my parade!'*

I knew instantly that we were gonna be friends, and it wasn't long before we were doing cabaret shows. There was Lee, Bella, a female lead singer who was all hands and no flair, and me. I was the backing singer. Bella didn't like me at all, nor I her. She was dull and pretentious; she fired me after the first few shows.

'She's deliberately upstaging me', she told Lee.

'I don't think there was anything deliberate about it', his brilliant reply.

'Oh NO! We've no piano!', I shout to my mother and Celia, who are on the steps, the day before the piano party. We'd completely forgotten we had given it back to my aunt.

'Aw No! Don't worry, I'll ask John to bring my piano down on the back of his truck', Celia tells my mother and me. 'Don't worry, he'll do it for me, I'll go round to him now.'

She kept her word, and on the morning of the party, she arrived on the back of a truck with the piano. As it crawled down Pearse Street she stood, played it and sang to the rapturous applause of drivers in the traffic and everyone on the whole street. She was phenomenal!

Friends and neighbours crammed the open parlours of our house in The Square that night, the 'hooley' was in full swing. Everyone 'did a turn'; acapella or accompanied, food, whiskey, wine, Guinness and brandy were taken. Celia and Maureen banged the hell out of the piano with their rumbustious duets. Lee slapped, smacked and bashed the keys, as he belted out one superb song after another. Lee could play anything, Cole Porter, Gershwin, Rogers & Hart, Hammerstein, Bernstein, Sondheim. Songs made famous by Ella, Sarah, Frank, Tony, Liza with a Z and Strei-sand with an S, as well as many others, filled our Square that night. I looked over at my formally shy mother, who didn't drink alcohol; she was dancing in hysterics laughing, enraptured by the mayhem and the madness that engulfed us. Our beautiful, ramshackle house was the scene for many a party over the years, Halloween, Christmas, birthdays, engagements and weddings. Magical times shared with family, friends, and neighbours, so many friends we often spilt on to the steps and revelled into the early morning.

An Incident

'Will you come up and do me hair for me on Friday? We're going up to the club to see Joe Dolan, do you wanna come? Did you ever see him? Ah jaysus he's great, you wanna see him singing, ah he's fantastic', Esther says as she Brassos the front door. 'Look at them gleaming, you can see your face in them.'

'I'm not going to Joe Dolan, but I'll do your hair for you', I say.

'Now don't let me down, don't make a fool of me, I'm warning you.' she says. 'I need me perm done, and me colour. Will you get them for me in town? I'll give you the money.'

'No, I don't want it', I tell her. 'I'll pay for it.'

'Are you sure now. I'll give you the money. Make sure and get them in Terry Sales do you hear me? Get the right one, do you hear me?', she says, 'Are you sure you have it?'

'Yes, yeah!', I tell her, 'I have it. I'll get it; don't worry, I'll get it for you.'

*   *   *

I thought it was her when I walked by Cleary's on O'Connell Street the following Thursday. I was on my way in to get a pair of gloves, to finish my look as a sexy goth. Even though Carly is only fourteen and I'm fifteen we

127

go to bars and clubs (though we don't drink alcohol) in town regularly. Like most of the people I know that live in town or near, it's nothing for us to be in town twice, three times a week. Clubs, and bars, like *The Apartment* or *The Harp* were for mainstreamers, though I liked them, we preferred alternative dives like *Bartley Dunnes*, *The William Tell* and *McGonagles*, frequented by goths, Cureheads, skinheads, mods, punks, gays, straights, and all kinds of loveable misfits.

'Boo!', I say into her ear. She's standing at the bus stop for the 22a. She's leaning on the handle of her trolley, her jacket thrown over the handle. Her shopping piled high inside, next to her portable oxygen tank.

'You're nearly after giving me a heart attack! Oh, it's very warm, isn't it? I'm sweating', she gasps and wipes her hand over her damp, shiny forehead.

'Where are you going?'

'In to buy a pair of black lace fingerless gloves for tonight', I tell her.

'You're mental', she laughs. 'Who you goin out with?'

'I'm going into McGonagles with me friends and me cousin, Sheelagh.'

'Where are YOU going?', I ask her.

'Nowhere. Home', she tells me. 'I was in Penneys getting a few pairs of pyjamas for the Christmas.'

'It's only August', I say. 'There's something wrong with you. Have you anything to do later?'

'No, nothing', she replies. 'Your Nanny, Ill be back at five and there's a dinner there for her, why?'

'Come into Cleary's with me. I'll get me gloves and we'll get the bus down to me Mams.'

'What about Bonnie?' Bonnie, her Yorkshire Terrier, a bow-wearing, vicious terror who continuously tries to bite my ankles, is her new baby.

'We'll ring Nanny and tell her to feed her. She'll be grand, come on.' I say dismissing her.

'Look who I found in town', I tell my mother.

'She dragged me down here Betty. She's a demon, wouldn't let me go home', she says to my mother, holding her chest, panting and collapsing onto the chair.

'Who are you telling', my mother says. 'Sit down, do you want to drink a water? I'll put on a cup of tea for us. Come ere Margret. Go to the shops for us will you, please, and get us a nice ham and cheese bread roll each and whatever you want. Do you want onions and tomatoes on yours, Esther?'

'Oh yeah, lovely Betty, thanks. Don't mind me, I needed to catch me breath.'

The cute little garden in the front basement of our Georgian house is bursting with beautiful herbs and flowers. There, my mother potters for hours singing, planting, pruning and culling, her straw hat shredded and plopped on her head. It's there I leave the two pals, drinking tea, eating and gossiping in the warm evening sunshine.

*   *   *

'What colour did you get me?', she asks, like it's a test.

'The one I always get you to cover your grey', I tell her. 'Deep copper red.'

'Good', she says. 'Where's the perm lotion?'

'Here, I have it here. It's in a box with the neutraliser', I tell her.

'We'll do the perm first', I say, 'Then we'll put the colour over it.'

'Is it alright to put them in together?', she asks me, her eyes narrow to scrutinise ...

'Yeah of course it is', I say. 'I do work in a hairdressers you know.' Though that was debatable. My father owned the hairdressers where I supposedly worked every Thursday, Friday, and Saturday. But a vast amount of that time, I could be found sauntering around town, having coffee, and pretending to get supplies. Though I did feel confident enough to take on a perm and a colour, I just wasn't entirely sure they could be done together. I brought rollers from the hairdressers as well as the papers for the tips of the hair, to stop it from being damaged; the consummate professional was I.

It wasn't long before I had an audience in my grandmother's front room. First, Phil arrived, then Mary, then Bridie, and then Vera to watch me effectuate my extensive skills. Coddle, bread, butter and tea, as well as many compliments were passed around.

'Good girdle yourself, isn't she great?', Vera says, rubbing her hands.

'You might be able to do mine? Can you do the streaks or highlights?', says Phil.

'Would my hair be nice permed?', asks Mary.

Knowing I was being watched, I carried out my job with great determination and with as much pomp and ceremony as was appropriate. Firstly, I used the section comb to get an even section of hair and then I took the paper to protect the ends of the hair and wrapped it neatly around the hair. Then I folded that onto the roller, rolling it down onto the scalp and fastening it with the elastic fastener. Then I applied lashings of perm lotion all over her head.

'Look at it, it's perfect, unbelievable', she's a great young one', Phil tells the group.

'Me scalp is burning me, give us a piece of wet tissue. She's scalding the head off me', Esther tells them.

'It always burns, perm lotion always burns', I tell her, 'Even in the hairdressers!'

'I'm only saying, I hope me hair doesn't fall out.' I see her winking at the others. 'Ah I'm only joking with yea', she says to me and smiles.

'Shush it won't, stop saying that.'

'Someone open that window please; the smell of this stuff is choking me', Esther says. 'Oh, jaysus me scalp is scalded off me! I'm serious, is it supposed to burn like this? When are you taking them out?'

'It's GRAND!', I say, losing patience with her. 'We're nearly finished, five more minutes and I'll rinse it.' I then rinse her hair, apply the neutraliser, then rinse it again so I can finally take out the rollers. But as I unwind the rollers, I notice instead of curls her hair is sticking up from her scalp, in places poker straight.

'What's it like? Did it take?', she asks me.

'Yeah, it's great' I tell her; 'It looks great.'

But to my horror, when I unwind the next roller, it breaks off from her scalp, with her hair still attached.

The sight of my face tells the tale, and my auntie Vera frantically mouths to me; 'Rinse it again, NOW.'

'I think I'll give it another rinse just to make sure all the lotion's out of it', I say to Esther, trying to downplay the urgency to get the potent lotion out of her hair.

'Why, is it alright?', she asks, her voice raised; she's slightly alarmed.

'No, it's grand, it's grand. I just want to rinse it a bit more,' I tell her, trying to remain calm.

'You're drowning me', she barks, bent over in the shower.

'What', I say, pretending not to hear her.

'I said your effin drowning me, I'm soaking wet, that's enough!', she screams at me.

'She's after drowning me in that shower, me drawers and all are soaking', she tells my aunts.

'Don't exaggerate', I tell her, 'Take off that sweatshirt. Here's a dry towel for you!'

'Nurse Ratched', she says. 'She's very rough. You couldn't open a salon. You're like a docker, you're too rough, the poor customers would never come back!' My aunts are in stitches.

I wasn't. I was gently patting the rollers dry with my heart in my mouth. I was unwinding the next roller at the crown of her head, when it slipped out of my hand, onto the floor and in between her feet, with her hair attached to it.

'Is that my hair on that fuckin roller, sweet Jesus, Mary and Joseph, me fuckin hair!!! What are you after doing to me? It's not funny, stop laughin, you wouldn't like it if it was your hair', she shouts at Vera.

'What are you after doing? Why is it breaking off!', she's now screaming at me.

'I don't know, I don't know', I say. 'It's in date. I checked it when I bought it, the perm lotion', I tell her panicking.

'Where did you get it?', she stares at me.

And all of a sudden, it dawns on me, my place of purchase may not have been the savviest decision I ever made, and I don't want to tell her.

'Where did you get it?', she says; 'Where did you buy it?' It wasn't like her, but she insists I answer.

'The, the, pound shop', I say.

I haven't even finished the sentence and my aunts are in hysterics. But I'm not and neither is Esther. I'd let her down, and the rest of them were laughing at her.

'I asked you had you got the money to buy it in *Terry Sales*, you said you had it. I wanted to give it to you.' Esther says, disgusted with me.

'I know', I say, ashamed. 'I should have bought it there, but I went out the night before and saw it in the pound shop for a pound; I checked the date, so I thought it'd be fine.'

My aunts are now roaring laughing.

This time Esther turns on them; 'Do yis think it's funny do yis? Get the fuck out! Go on, everyone of yis, get out!'

'What, we can't help it, we're only laughing cos she said the pound shop, sorry', Vera says.

'Ah there's no need for that', says Phil.

'Out!', Esther shouts; 'Jeering and sneering me in me own home? Yis can get out, get out!'

Bridie pleads with Esther, 'We didn't mean any harm, it was just when she said the pound shop, we couldn't help it.'

With that, my auntie Phil lets out a howling roar and runs to the door, crossing her legs like a knotted spider. 'I'll see you later Esther, I'll see, I'm sorry, I'll see you later.'

We can hear her screaming and laughing as she runs out of the gate. I too, want to run out the door, but I can't. I have to stay, face Esther, and try to fix her hair. She stands staring at the remaining three until they lean and scrape their bags and coats and squirm out the door.

'I'll take the rest of them out I tell her, hopefully, it was just that one; it was in the longest. Don't worry it's on the crown of your head, we can cover it. I don't think we'll do the colour today', I babble, trying to say anything to relieve the awful tension in the air.

'Do you think?', she says in a low voice and doesn't look at me.

'One more roller with her hair attached breaks off, but it was a thin strand, at the crown of her head, so I managed to take it out and hide it. There were also some fine broken strands that were sticking up too. Thank God she had a lot of hair because she had a one-inch square bald patch at the crown of her head. She then puts her finger to it and tugs the hairs around it. 'It's not as bad as I thought it was, if I blow dry over it, you won't see it.'

'That's what I'm doing', I tell her. 'Will I trim it for you?'

'No thanks!', she says, 'No thanks very much You've done enough, I'm lucky I'm not fuckin baldy!'

'I know, sorry', I say; 'I feel so bad. I should have got it in Terry Sales.'

'It's ok, it doesn't matter, you didn't mean it', she says, softening to her old self again.

'Now see, it looks gorgeous', I say, which it did to a point.

'I thought it would have been curlier', she says.

'Yeah, it's not so much a corkscrew as a body wave', I say, regaining my confidence.

'You'd say mass', she says. 'Get me the tongs under the stairs, can you manage to tongs it?', she asks me sarcastically; 'Without fuckin scalding me?'

'Yeah, of course I can.'

*   *   *

A few weeks after the perm incident, I was in my Nanny's house on a Saturday afternoon, eating my dinner and minding my own business when Esther tells me, 'We're going up to the north. Are you coming?'

'Yeah, come, we're going Christmas shopping', Vera says.

'C'mon for a laugh', says Phil, sucking on her cigarette till her eyes nearly cross.

'What are yis buying clothes, or messages?', I ask.

'Christmas shopping, biscuits, cakes, drink, sweets and if you see clothes, you can get them as well; you might see something nice no one else has', says Esther.

'But it's only September?', I say.

'I know, but Christmas is only twelve weeks away, the time is flying in! I heard the bargains up there are brilliant! Margie Robberts got the washing powder and all the selection boxes, the boxes of sweets up there, the works, 'for nothin!' We'll bring the trollies and get the train up and down. It'll be great craic, anyway, will we go up?', Phil begs me.

'Up the north' didn't sound like a great prospect to me.

'Are yis sure?'

This was September 1988, long before the *Good Friday Agreement,* and 'the troubles' were still raging; people dying on both sides. It was tragically sad, the suffering of the people in Northern Ireland. Bombings, raids and riots were still a part of everyday life. All of which, I believe, my aunts never gave a second thought to, they were too sweet, too innocent, too kind. They were more concerned with the price of *USA* biscuits, boxes of *Quality Street, Cadbury's Roses,* the price of *Major* cigarettes and *Smirnoff* vodka.

The following Thursday morning, we arrived at Connelly station. Cans of coke, orange, foil-wrapped sandwiches as high as any mountain, bars of chocolate, and enough crisps 'in case we're hungry' to feed a battalion were packed for the journey.

'You didn't put salad cream on them, did you Esther? I told you I didn't like salad cream.', Vera says.

'Well don't eat them then!', Esther's response.

'Who has the ham sandwiches? Did you boil that ham yesterday, are they fresh?', Phil asks Mary, giving me a pirate's wink.

'Go long and ask MY arse!', Mary tells her, 'Why didn't you make your own!'

'Pass me one over there please' says Phil 'an I'll see what it's like.'

'Remind me not to forget to get me cigarettes, twenty *Major's* half the price up there compared to Dublin, isn't that hard to believe?', Esther tells me, reviewing her list, an arrangement of rare chicken scrawl indecipherable to the naked eye.

'I'll try and get two hundred, the voka (vodka), 'Macardi' (*Bacardi*) brandy, *USA* biscuits, *Quality Street*. We'll see how much the *Roses* are here; Rita Matthews told me the 'minerills' are for nothing, so we'll get some of them as well. Your ma told me to pick her up the *Quality Street*, the *USA* biscuits, the *Roses,* and whatever else I think, and you carry them in your trolley, right', Esther tells me, puffing on a cigarette and waving away the smoke with almost no effect.

'Tell me if you see your man coming', the conductor.

After three hours, we arrive and disembark the train. We get a taxi into the town centre but are shocked by the armed British soldiers patrolling the city, brandishing their weapons.

'Very serious lookin aren't they?', Phil remarks, 'There you are gorgeous' she says with a cackle to a very stern-looking soldier.

'Yeah, there's no craic in them; look at the face on them!', interjects Vera.

'Shut up yous!', says Bridie, 'What do yis think the troubles are, a party? They'd blow your brains out?'

'Oh, Mammy', says Esther, 'And we're only here to buy biscuits and sweets!'

Three of the six soldiers walking to the side and behind us, look no more than eighteen years old. It seems our Irish accents are attracting a bit of attention.

'They're only kids; look at them, God love them, they're someone's child', Mary says under her breath.

'That's right', says Bridie, 'Some poor woman's child.'

'Aw quick! Look!', says Phil; 'There's a *Crazy Prices*!'

And with that, we run through the *Crazy Prices* doors, trolleys in tow, like a shower of lunatics, on day release from an asylum.

'Quick, there look, the coke is only 50p for two litres!', says Phil to me; 'Get five!'

'Look at that', says Mary, 'The vodka is only £7 a litre, so is the brandy, and the *Bacardi* look, so is whiskey, ah that's for nothin. You couldn't pass that! You couldn't pass it!'

'I think I'll get three bottles of *Bacardi* and three bottles of vodka; it means I have them in for the Christmas', says Mary.

'You will alright, you and her (pointing at Phil) will have every drop of that gone by Halloween', jeers Bridie.

'No, I'm serious, it's for the Christmas. Anyway, what am I givin me senses to you for?', says Mary, packing three bottles of vodka, three bottles of *Bacardi* and two bottles of *Jameson* into her trolley.

The price of every item from shampoo to nappies was discussed, dissected, contrasted and compared to the prices 'at home.' Not a bargain escaped their crafty eyes.

'I'm exhausted', says Esther. 'We'll have to sit down again and have a bit of lunch. Did you get everything you wanted?', she asks me.

'Yep' I tell her. 'I got *Quality Street*, *Cadburys Roses*, *USA* biscuits, selection boxes, vodka, *Jameson*, brandy and washing powder for me ma.' She'll be delighted.

138

'Yeh come on', says Phil, putting her arm around me. 'We'll get fish and chips, will we?'

'And mushy peas', says Vera; 'Don't the English love mushy peas with their fish n chips?'

'And then we'll get cream cakes', I tell them.

'And a nice pot of tea', says Esther.

We went to a large cafe inside the shopping centre, dragging our bursting trolleys and were looking at the food menu when Esther looks up; 'Don't say anything, but them soldiers are following us.'

'Don't be foolish, Esther', says Mary; 'They're not minding us. Jaysus they're probably getting something to eat.'

'They are not', Vera says, dipping a *Mars* bar in her tea; 'They're not minding us.'

Bridie looks around; 'She's right, they're the same young fellas, the same ones that followed us around the street and supermarket.'

'Oh Mammy, me nerves are gone', Esther says, taking a large bite out of a coffee slice.

'With a bit a luck, they'll strip search us!', Phil laughs.

'That's not funny. Stop looking they're not minding us', Mary says.

'I need to get me smokes', says Esther.

'So do I.', says Phil. 'Stay there I'll get them. How many do you want?'

'Two hundred! Now get me Major, don't get me anything I don't know, do you hear me?'

'I will, I will, I heard yea!', says Phil.

Another two pots of tea are finished and after half an hour Esther jumps up.

'Ah here, where's she, I'm going to look for her, we'll miss the train if she doesn't hurry up. Is that her?' There was a red dot in the distance with a head of blond 'streaks', laughing, joking, with what looked like a gang of women.

'Aw it is her, the headcase she'd talk to anyone. Did you get me smokes; did you get me smokes?', Esther stage whispers to Phil for the whole shopping centre to hear.

'Yeh, Phil is nodding. I have them here!' Phil reaches inside her sports jacket to retrieve said two hundred Major, but before she can, she's lifted off the floor and pushed towards the wall by two of the young soldiers. The ones Esther said were following us.

As we run towards her, we hear the soldiers roar, 'Irish', 'Smoke', and 'Bomb.'

'What ave you got, what ave you got there, search her', one of them shouts. Four more appear, pointing guns.

'Leave me alone, leave me alone, they're me cigarettes, What's wrong with cigarettes? I'm allowed buy cigarettes!', roars Phil with her nose to the wall and her legs apart. She's patted down by one of the younger ones.

'That's all she has sir, cigarettes', the soldier tells the more serious, more senior soldier that has just joined the group.

'What are you doing here?', he asks Phil.

'Minding me own business, that's what I'm doing!', she tells him.

'What does it look like she's doing? Shopping, shoppin for the Christmas!' Esther fires her words: if they could kill, they would have.

'What does it look like I'm doing? Getting me Christmas shopping, buying sweets and biscuits, and

140

getting the drink in for the Christmas?', Phil says, her face red with fright and rage.

Then Bridie, tall, blonde, and elegant makes a run at them, she looks like a model, has the heart of a lion and can fight like a man.

'Put your hands on her again and I'll knock you out. Yis dirty looking fucking eejits yis. Go way yis fools! Grabbing a woman minding her own business, doing her shoppin.' She turns to the younger one who grabbed Phil, 'You louser yeh. You little pup yeh. Have you no manners!'

'I'm sorry madam, I am sorry about that', the good-looking, senior soldier apologises.

'Sorry my arse', Bridie answers him as we walk away to retrieve our abandoned shopping; 'Sorry my arse!'

'That was your fault', says Phil to Esther; 'roaring about smokes all over the shopping centre.'

'I was only asking you did you get them; I didn't mean any harm', Esther says to her, grey in the face.

'Your false teeth were chatterin in your mouth and you weren't even speakin', Vera jeers Phil.

'It's not funny' Phil answers, wiping the sweat from her brow, 'I nearly wet meself with the fright.'

'Well at least you got strip searched', laughs Mary. 'Not strip searched exactly, but your man the older fella was gorgeous wasn't he, I'd have asked him for his number if he wasn't such a fuckin eejit!'

'Couldn't bless himself.' Phil finally smiles and gives us all permission to laugh.

'Come on, we can't miss this train. Oh Mammy, I'd never come up here again, not for all the tea in China', Esther says, and we all agree.

All the way home, rare nuggets of wisdom are exchanged between these glorious women; 'It's an awful kip isn't it', 'I wouldn't take a house up there if they were given them away.' 'Thank God we live in Dublin.'

Commiserations and sandwiches are also shared with the old man whose daughter has 'the misfortune to be stuck up in the God-forsaken kip.' Our hearts temporarily break 'for the poor Irish livin up there', but concessions are made ... and it is agreed by one and all 'that the stuff is for nothin!'

Nights on Broadway

I was twenty two years old when the yellow cab drove over the Brooklyn Bridge into Manhattan. It was the beginning of September and the multicoloured lights from the city sprayed across the evening sky. The sun, going down and electric orange, lit my soul. The warm breeze blowing in my face, the sound of horns, hustle, bustle and people shouting. This was New York in the mid 1990s, and it was the bomb!

I'd met Mat in Dublin. He was doing a show in the Abbey Theatre. He was an actor and I thought I was in love. After much letter writing and long-distance calling, it was decided I would move to New York. A friend of a friend from home, Caitríona had invited me to stay at her place in Brooklyn, but I went to see Mat first. Mat's apartment building, an old brownstone on West 36th, street and 11th Avenue, buckled under the grim shade. I paid for the cab and Mat appeared. He was smiling. It was great to see him and to finally arrive in New York. I was so excited I couldn't wait to go out. Out, out, out into the chaos that was New York City, skipping up Broadway, happy, free, I just knew this was for me.

I loved Hell's Kitchen, the restaurants, streets and bars, lively, exciting, wild, vibrant, the people loud, glad, mad and bad! Images crashed, flashed, popped, intoxicating, exhilarating, relentless!

The next day, I called my friend and in her newly

acquired New York accent, she told me I couldn't stay with her as she hadn't asked her roommate. 'Sure, you can stay with yer man', she said. I was pissed off, raging. Cohabitation wasn't part of the plan but needs must. Mat was kind and generous, but I had to get a job and fast. I'd arrived with $500, and it was nearly gone.

'Here, take that and pawn it.' My mother had said. 'Make sure you get it back for me.' Generous to a fault, she handed me her engagement ring to get to New York. A large solitaire diamond set high in gold, that was worth at least £5,000; I got £500 for it and lost the ticket. Mat had been out of town for the previous two weeks on an acting job. I'd been living on a large bag of boiled rice and a jar of sweet and sour sauce watered down until it disappeared.

I walked up and down every street until I came to an Irish bar on Restaurant Row. *Malin's Tavern* was a rustic Aladdin's cave, delightful, demented, delicious and de-lovely. There, candles, old books, paintings and trinkets filled every nook and cranny. An eloquently dressed mannequin sat in the corner enjoying her tea and a copper bar sparkled under twinkling lights that winked at my eyes.

'Where you from?', the owner asked in an Irish accent. He was grey-haired, tall, in his early fifties and looked me up and down. 'Dublin', I told him in my cheeriest voice, 'and I've loads of experience.' I lied.

Sean, the owner, was cunning, cheap, brilliant, ruthless, charming, funny, artistic and kind. On my first day he enlightened me as to kitchen procedure.

'Listen, that's not how we do it here. There're little

144

children starving all over the world and it's like, a sin, to waste food. So, we recycle ketchup and mayonnaise, for example, if there's sauce over from a meal, scrape it into a new plastic container and put it in the fridge, like so', he informed me as he carried out that exact act. I was too desperate and hungry to argue about the Health and Safety implications but threw them in the bin when his back was turned.

'We sell twenty six different types of beer and ales on tap. Ales being our speciality. We're known worldwide for our fine ales and beers', he says as he points to a small menu to be placed on each table. However, he forgot to clarify there were only six taps and it was up to the skill of the bartender on the day to pass these beers off as their advertised names. Mixing dark ales, light ales and beers to create magical potions that cast spells on unsuspecting customers took a particular type of wizardry.

Sean had a voice serious and low with a soft Cavan lilt and when he talked it was with hypnotic effect. He could make the most outrageous lies, atrocious acts seem plausible, even acceptable, with his sweet voice and sincere delivery. I knew he could be a dishonest scoundrel, but he made me laugh and that was good enough for me!

Being the halfwit that I am, I have observed that I am willing to throw all good moral standing out the window, for someone who makes me laugh, anyone. Sean reminded me of an ex-boyfriend, hilariously funny and a lying bastard all at the same time. Though his character was distinctly lowly and flawed, the fault was clearly mine. I was a nuisance to my own progress and enjoyed every minute of it!

Sean didn't like people sitting for hours over one drink. He was constantly insulting and ejecting customers from his premises and would instruct me to do the same. I would run from him, hide in corners and try not to laugh. My introduction to this procedure was swift, the language plain.

'See that c**t over there, well he's sipping a beer the last four fucking hours. Throw him out! Tell him I need that table.'

If I was unsuccessful in my endeavour, he would go over to the said customer and, in the sweetest Irish lilt, explain.

'Excuse me, excuse me sir, I need that table you're sitting at. Would you mind finishing up that beer please? See, I have to pay a little thing called taxes to the city of New York every year and I can't tell them I had people like you in my bar. Spending no money. See, they wouldn't believe me, they'd call me a liar, and throw me in the county jail. So, would you mind finishing that beer and getting the fuck out of my bar! You're sitting there the last four hours and I'm not running a charity, so would you like fuck off, … please?'

The customer, usually horrified, would leave in complete disgust. 'And don't come back', he'd say, as they stormed out the door. With faux innocence, quizzical eyebrows, hands outstretched and smothering a laugh, he'd shrug his shoulders, 'Unbeleeeeivable some people! Unbelieeeevable? And HE'S annoyed!'

Sean was insane but would also go out of his way for you too. He had huge respect for artists and musicians.

When Barbra Streisand was playing in Madison Square Garden, I went to him.

'Sean, I need a loan please! I have to see Barbra Streisand tonight! I've no money, I need a loan, the tickets are $2,000 each!' He grabbed his chest and burst out laughing, 'Are you fucking serious, two fuckin thous ...'

'But I only want $300 off you! I'll go down there and do me best to get in! And the night off as well! I adore her!' He got my shift covered, gave me $350 and sent me on my way. I queued for six hours until they sold the last tickets for a discounted $1,500. The promoter told another woman and me, not to move. He had already offered us the discounted tickets. I told him I couldn't afford it. He came back and asked us how much money we had. I told him $300. He sold us the last two tickets for Barbra Streisand in New York for $300! The next morning, our picture was on the cover of the New York Times.

It was a magical night; I pushed nearer the front and cried the whole time. Barbra was beautiful, in excellent voice and high camp as ever; 'All my friends are here tonight. Please welcome the wonderful Marvin Hamlisch, Tony Bennet, Isabella Rossellini, my manager Marty Erlichman ...'

*   *   *

It was a week before Christmas and me and Rich, the bartender, were heading to Rudy's for a drink. Sean collared us outside. He was drunk but deadly serious, 'Sheila, Sheila, Rich, listen, we need to do a bit of carol singing, so can you gather the girls and guys together and sing some carols? There are some beautiful Christmas carols, you know, stuff like 'Hark the Herald Angels Come', or 'Silent Night' You know one of them? It's such a wonderful time of year and a time for Christmas cheer.'

'Hark the Herald Angels COME!', I say, laughing so hard I hardly notice the poor homeless man beside us.

'Excuse me, sir', the man says.

Sean ignores him and continues, 'You know, in the spirit of this beautiful season, people love to hear Christmas carols; it's a spiritual thing, you know?'

Again, the homeless man interrupts us, 'I'm sorry sir, but I'm homeless and hungry. Can you help a brother please sir? I'm really hungry.'

'No', Sean tells him.

'Please', the man persists.

With that, Sean turns around and says, 'Listen can you not see I'm talking here; would you ever fuck off! Can you not see I'm having a conversation here with this young lady? Stop interrupting me ye c**t ye!'

Then without missing a beat, he turns back to us, 'Anyway, as I was saying, it's such a beautiful time of year, and such a spiritual thing, isn't it? Singing these beautiful songs, it's a time for giving. Organise it. I'm off now, goodnight.' Pouted lipped and glassy eyed he saunters off, briefcase in hand, brogues in the snow ...

We apologise to the homeless man and give him $20. Walking down the street, we can't stop laughing, not at the homeless man of course but at Sean missing the whole point, or just dismissing it outright. This was Sean Malins esquire, at his best, at his worst, and at your service. An original, a go-getter, a comic, a rogue, an artist, a legend.

Mat and I were living together for a few months, but

things were strained. He wasn't working, and I was paying the bills. He started drinking in a bar on 9th Avenue where the bartender Sam, took a shine to him. She was from New Jersey and rough as a badger's arse. I had an idea something was going on, but I knew it was, when he asked me to move out. I went ballistic but had no proof they were having an affair. Then, one night I waited as she shut the bar and there lurking like a snake in the shadows was Mat. He greeted her with a kiss.

'You fucking lying bastard, you', I screamed. 'Going off with that hag, how dare you!' I bounced his pager off his head, and it smashed to the ground.

'That's it', he screamed, 'get your shit and get out of my apartment tonight.'

'I'm leaving anyway asshole!', I said, and with that I rang my friend Ursula from the bar and stayed at hers for a night and for the next few weeks. I stayed on other friends couches too.

When ringing home to check in, I did what I thought all decent daughters should do: lie through my teeth! Telling the truth unthinkable...imagine the call: 'Hi Mam. You know the guy you didn't know I was living with? Well, he threw me onto the street at 1 in the morning. I'm in a shit-hole area of Manhattan where the only decent people are transsexual hookers and crack addicts! Oh yeah and tonight, after work, I take the train at 2am to another shitty area in Jamaica, Queens, to sleep on another friend's couch. I don't have the money for a deposit, and I think I'm dying of a broken heart.' I wasn't dying so much of a broken heart as a broken ego. I didn't cope very well with the decision not being mine. The feeling that I was drowning and couldn't find the bank beneath my feet haunted me day and night.

I buy a phone card and use a pay phone on the street to call Esther and Nanny every couple of weeks, just to hear their sweet voices. Nanny's still never in.

'What's it like in America, is it nice? Are the people nice to you? Won't you be careful? Maybe I'll come and visit you? Would I like it? Do you ever see any film stars?', Esther asks.

'No, I never see any. The people are lovely, but I'm going to a Broadway show the weekend and I'm going to meet Gregory Peck backstage!', I tell her and it was true.

'*Atticus*', he played '*Atticus*' in *To Kill a Mockingbird*, did you ever see it? It's a great film. Won't you tell me all about it', she says.

'I will, I promise. I'm working in an Irish bar. Everyone's lovely, they're all very nice, I'm ok it's very safe. I have to go', I tell her.

'I love you; I miss you', she says.

'Me card is running out, I ... '. Click.

My work, friends and wine kept me busy, and I soon move into a two-bedroom apartment on 43rd Street between 8th and 9th Avenue with Josephine and Eve. They are my Mormon friends. They are a scream, especially Josephine. She's an absolute lunatic, the epitome of a crazed, insecure, insane and deranged actress, and I fucking love her! She'd been a chubby teenager and now works out like an Olympian. She spends most days looking at herself in the mirror, asking me if she's fat.

'Am I fat? Do you think I look fat in this? Do I look fat to you? Do I look like a skinny girl, that used to be fat? Or do I look like a fat girl that could be thinner?', she goes on and on. She's having her voice trained and spends most mornings vocalising in the living room; 'Vavavavavavavav vaaaaaa, mememeememememe, me me me meeeeeeeee.'

'Shut up Josephine, it's nine in the morning and I worked all night', I bang on the door and call out through the crack.

'I'm just vocalising, can you watch my audition piece, please?', she asks.

'No', I say.

'Please?', she begs. I always give in. She then shows me her piece. She is brilliant, talented and usually ends her audition in bits, sobbing on the floor!

'Did you like it?', she asks me like a child.

'It's alright', I torment her. Her face drops. I torment her some more, then relent and tell her she is a genius. She was, is, one of the most talented people I have ever met, and I adore her.

Eve, her cousin, is on tour with *Kiss of the Spider Woman*. She's a brilliant dancer, beautiful and down to earth. Check-shirt, crooked smile and beer in hand, she observes her cousin's madness with wry humour. On the fire escape, basking in the sun, we smoke like chimneys, swig beers and talk about men. Robert is Josephine's best friend and will soon be mine. He's Mexican, gay and acting with Vanessa Redgrave and Patrick Stuart in *Shakespeare in the Park*. If we aren't working, we go to Rudy's bar, dance on tables, drink and eat free hotdogs all night. A proper den of iniquity, a place frequented by addicts, locals and hookers. Fucked up and fabulous, just like us! Some nights, we go downtown to Time or Temple Bar, Swift or Bowery. Wherever we go, we have a blast. On the way home, we chat with the transsexual hookers who parade themselves up and down our street, we share cigarettes and stories. Francesca's my friend. On occasion, they bend over and tuck themselves under, in our mirrored door.

This too is New York, funky, fruity ... faaaaantaaaastic!

Standing on the street on 9th Avenue hailing a cab on a summer's evening, MAC make up, big hair and a tiny waist, the warm wind in my face, high heels and a gold clutch. I feel like I'm in a movie; I'm having the time of my life.

I take voice, dance and audition when I can. One spring morning, I found myself outside ABC studios. I'd gotten an audition for the daytime soap opera, '*One Life to Live*' One of the lead actors, Thorsten Kaye, a gent, drank in *Malin's* and told me about the audition for the part of an Irish maid, 'Kathleen.' I auditioned and got the part. There was only one small catch. I'd overstayed my visa and was illegal. In the spirit of youth, and not to miss an opportunity, I said 'fuck it', and went right in. The receptionist pointed me to an office where I was supposed to give my visa details, bank account information, and social security number. I gave my own bank details but borrowed a friend's social security number and changed the last few digits. The guy checking my details was officious and towering. He asked for my visa. I began to search my purse, jacket and bag. Casually at first, then frantically.

'Oh my God, I can't find it.' I try to cry and am soon in floods of tears. 'I can't find my visa; I had it earlier, I must have lost it. I can't believe this! I'm sorry! I'm sorry. I'll go home. Maybe I left it there.'

'No. No, it's fine, you need to go to hair and makeup. Just bring it in the next time', he says. There, in that office I pulled one of my best performances out of the bag, if not my visa!

Hair, make-up, lights, camera, action. I was 'Kathleen from Kilkea.' Nervous as I was, I was well prepared and did a great job, if I do say so myself. Sean threw a party for the airing of the first episode in the bar and made everyone except me pay for the drinks!

Shortly after my best friend Nuala came to visit. We went out every night and drank like fish. One night in a bar, we met a bunch of guys. A grey-haired Freddy took a shine to Nuala. I thought I was hanging out with the cast of *Goodfellas*, though these guys were Greek. They told us they ran casinos and sold slot machines. They were great fun and polite, so being the sociable young ladies we were, we accepted an invitation to the opening of a club downtown. We drank copious amounts of champagne and danced all night. On the way home, we had a big breakfast in Galaxy Diner and Nuala promptly vomited it all up outside our front door. We woke up the next day to a ranting and a rightly furious Josephine screaming at the top of her lungs.

'You are alcoholic Irish drunks; why do you drink so much, alcoholic Irish drunks.' I threw a shoe at my door in protest, 'That wasn't us, so shut up Josephine. It must have been the neighbour. How dare you speak to us like that. That's outrageous! We want an apology', I demand as we giggle and wriggle off the hook.

I was still working at *Malin's Tavern* and making a fortune. I worked for $2 an hour and lived off my tips. I had drawers full of money and spent like a Rockefeller. Casts from Broadway shows came to the bar, including the cast from Miss Saigon. One evening, I was tidying up outside in the beer garden when I heard a jolly voice laughing. I felt a man watching me. He raised his hand to get my attention, 'May I have four Amstel beers please?' I brought him the beers. 'What's your name and where are you from?', he asked. I told him it was none of his business. He laughed. 'Can I buy you a drink?'

'Sure', I replied.

'No not now', he said, 'another time, here's my number, call me, What's your name?'

'Sheila'

'Ok, well why don't you call me, Sheila? I'd really like it if you did', he smiled, and wow did he have the most beautiful smile. His face was open and kind. He was the manager of The Broadway Theatre. Nuala giggled as I rang his office and left a voice message.

'At least he'll bring us out, even if you don't like him', she excitedly shrieked. I agreed. He called me a couple of hours later and said he'd take me out that night.

'Alright, but my friend has to come too', I informed him. It was a summer's evening in Manhattan, the sun was hot and burning as we sipped our wine on the fire escape. We heard a horn beep outside the apartment. I looked down, and there he was, suited and booted, standing against a red sports car. I shouted to him, 'I love New York!'

'Me too!', he laughed, his big loud, hearty laugh. We

ran down the stairs, drove downtown and had the best night ever. My life has been blessed with angels; Michael was one. Easy nights and cocktails in dimly lit bars. Owners of little restaurants who knew his name, Nell's on 14th Street, Temple Bar and The Russian Tea Room. We worshipped at the temple that was Manhattan and he, himself, was a native New Yorker.

It was coming up to Christmas. I'd been in New York for two years and I missed my family. I decided to take a chance and go home to Dublin for Christmas. I knew there was a possibility I wouldn't get back into the States, but I thought it unlikely. I told Michael my plan and he was worried. He tried to discourage me, but I was going anyway. He told me he'd be waiting for me when I got back. If I got back …

I flew back to Dublin Christmas week. I arrived like Joan Collins on the set of *Dynasty*. Fur hat, sheepskin coat, diamond earrings, very long nails and an attitude that would make Imelda Marcos look sweet. I thought I was the bomb, and I wasn't wrong. My mother met me at the front door: 'I'm delighted to see you; the hall, stairs and landings have to be mopped. There's plenty of work to be done this week.' Family are always the first to boot you off your pedestal; the novelty, that was me, wore off pretty quickly.

'This is not a hotel, while you're home you can pull your weight. I need your help. It's Christmas week', my mother reminds me.

'I'm going up to see Esther and Nanny first. I'll do it when I get back!'

'You're like a movie star', Esther tells me when I walk

into the house; she grips me in a hug, and kisses me. 'We'll go up to the Transport Club tonight so everyone can see you. Mammy, look at her; isn't she only gorgeous?'

My Nanny gives me a big hug and a kiss; 'Don't mind that, looks don't boil the pot! Are you home for long? How's your mother? I've green scapulars here for you, put them on you and bless yourself. I'm going to mass. I'll see you when I come back.'

'Nanny' I laugh, 'what about the new scarf I bought you? Do you want to wear it now?'

'No, wait till I have me hair done and I'll wear it to mass on Sunday, it's beauchiful!', she closes the door.

'Tell me about your man, are you alright now?', Esther asks me, a worried look on her face.

'Yes', I tell her. 'I'm going out with a new fella, he's lovely, mad about me, he manages the Broadway Theatre!'

'Good', she says, 'I was worried about you, don't ever waste your life on a man who doesn't want you, like I wasted mine.' I kiss her on the head.

'Have you got your colour. Come on and I'll put it in for you?', I tell her.

'Ok.' she smiles. 'Thanks for the beautiful ring, it's gorgeous; you shouldn't have done that', she says proudly as she sits enchanted by the ring I'd just given her.

'It's a real diamond', I tell her.

'I know!', she says, 'Wait till I show the rest of them, they'll be raging!'

We giggle.

I'd brought presents home for everyone and went out every night, but after a week at home, I was over it. I couldn't wait to get back to New York and out of the house. On the morning I was leaving Carly was standing on the stairs crying.

'What's the matter with you?', I say.

'I can't believe you're leaving, going back to New York. I wish I was going with you. I hate it here', she cries. She'd gone to New York at seventeen and couldn't get another visa.

'I don't blame you', I say. 'Dublin's an absolute dump. I feel sorry for you.' With that, I air kiss her and the rest of my family, wave goodbye and race to the airport.

The flight seemed longer than usual. I barely slept with excitement. Michael was meeting me there. The plane touched down in JFK. Well prepared with my answers and confident they wouldn't suspect I had overstayed my visa; I joined the queue for Immigration. The interrogation began, 'Name? Address? Reason for travelling? How long was your last visit to the United States? What do you work at? How long do you plan on staying?' I thought I had answered all of the questions correctly.

'We have no record of you leaving the United States after your last visit. Did you just leave before Christmas and go home for the holidays?', says the stony-faced cool-eyed immigration officer.

'No, no', I answer. 'I haven't been here in two years. I'm just going on holidays.' 'Really?', the officer asks, 'then you won't mind if I go through your wallet, will you?'

'No', I say, my heart sinking. He took out my wallet and searched through the slip and zip pockets. He slowly pushed a receipt across the desk and in front of my eyes. It was from Macy's, where I'd bought Christmas presents for my family. The date at the top, the 10th of December. The jig, as they say, was up! The cat, out of the bag, and I was fucked! I was refused entry and escorted by an armed guard to a holding area.

'You will be put on the next flight back to Dublin', he said. The death knell tolled. Before I left the airport, I called Michael and told him what had happened.

'Come to the glass partition', he said. I walked over to a glass wall, and there he was standing with a huge bunch of flowers, devastated, sobbing.

'Why, why did you go home? My heart is broken', he mouthed. We both stood there crying. Him over me, me over New York, until a security guard told me I had to get back to the holding area.

'I have to go, Michael. I'll call you when I get back', I mimed. I arrived back in Dublin at my mother's front door. Fur hat crooked on my head, black mascara running down my face, fake nails bitten and my tail firmly between my legs. Carly opened our front door.

'I was deported', I sobbed.

'What'? she laughed. 'Now Sheila', she said, 'I feel sorry for you!'

And who could blame her ...

A 'Damned!'

'That's disgusting!', he said in his Dutch accent. Peter was the brother of my best friend Elsa, and we were at a dinner party in her sister Katherine's apartment.

I had just put my fork into the main dish and picked out a lump of chicken, stuffing it in my face. I was about to do it again when he barked.

'How dare you put your fork into that dish, TWICE! Other people have to eat, you know!' We'd been out the night before, and I was dying of a hangover. Sweating, I asked myself why I was at this stupid dinner party and not in my bed eating *Monster Munch* and reading the *Enquirer* like a normal person!

I was mortified, red-faced and startled; I stuttered 'Oh I'm so sorry, I wasn't thinking, I,I,I …' He suddenly burst out laughing, 'I'm only joking with you!!'

I was annoyed, red-faced and embarrassed. I told him to 'Shut up.' My hands shaking, my nerves frayed. I was in Amsterdam visiting my friends, the Deckers. Two sisters, half Dutch, half Irish and half mental. They had returned to Amsterdam, having spent five years living in Dublin. Elsa and Katherine had that crazy Irish gene. They loved a bit of madness and were brilliantly wild. I'd arrived in Amsterdam two days before for the Queen's birthday, Queens Day, and had been drunk ever since.

I was staying with Elsa in her little flat, east of the city centre. This vibrant neighbourhood, mostly Turkish and Moroccan, was bustling with ethnic food, clothes, and people. Elsa's flat was sweet, small, spotless, and organised, with big windows opening onto the street. The Dutch have a way of mastering small spaces. I had a way of upending them, turning her cute flat into a den of complete and utter squalor.

She was an excellent host, extremely kind and generous. After two crazy days of drinking and dancing… for the queen, you understand, Katherine decided to host a dinner party. I was so tired I didn't want to go, but Elsa insisted. After a quick shower, I put new makeup on, over old, and backcombed my hair. Too lazy to brush it.

Katherine's apartment was on the very fashionable Prinsengracht. We arrived and climbed the steep stairs. Her apartment was bright, white, trendy and very spacious. A beautiful glass and steel odd-shaped designer table centred the room. While sideboards, hanging chandelier, candelabras, original artwork, and sculptures decorated the outskirts. A large bed lay softly tucked up three stairs behind a white half-wall, before the rounded window at the end of the room tipped over the stunning canal.

The breeze gently waved the summer evening muslin curtains as we entered the room, the large windows opened on the balcony. Jazz was soothing the guests, chatting, and drinking. A casual, warm, atmosphere laughing, greeting, kissing, and shaking of hands. Then a man walked into the room, shaved head, medium height, and beautiful green eyes.

'This is my brother Peter', said Elsa. 'Hello', he smiled. 'In Holland, we give three kisses', then kissed me three times. He forgot to tell me that only applied when you know someone very well. They were laughing.

'Very funny', I said, as I sat back down.

'Can I sit beside you for dinner?', he whispered.

'Sure', I said. I really wasn't paying him much attention. We started to eat dinner, drink wine, tell stories and chat, I was having a great time.

'Will you scratch my back?', he asked me in his thick Dutch accent, pointing to his back. 'No!', I said, 'are you crazy? I'm not scratching your back; how dare you! I don't even know you.' He giggled 'Oh, I see you are very stuffy; you think you're great. You really love yourself, don't you!'

'Whatever! Shut up!', I continue to eat.

His eyes, kind, sad and serious, looked straight into mine and in a very low voice, he whispered.

'Hey, hey ... I think you're great; I really love the way you are. I also like your red hair.' Taken aback and touched by his kind words, I say absolutely nothing and look into his eyes. The strangest feeling comes over me; I feel nervous, my face is red, my knees are shaking. His shoulder and arm are pressed into mine, his green eyes burning through the side of my face.

Everyone in the room disappeared into the walls. I was sitting there thinking, 'This man is mad; what the hell is he talking about? I've only just met him an hour ago.' But the other side of my brain was on fire, curious, terrified, captivated. Did he have a girlfriend? Why do I feel this chemistry, this electricity, this knowing, when I talk to him? How long is he staying tonight? What's happening to me?

'We're going to a bar down the road', Elsa announces. We pile down Katherine's tiny, steep stairs and begin to walk down the road towards the bar.

'I'm not going', Peter says, slightly annoyed, slightly drunk. 'She's going to get me into trouble', he nods at me. 'You might be a witch', he continued.

'No, no, no', everyone said together, 'you can't go home.' I said nothing; I just looked at him blankly and shrugged my shoulders as if I didn't care if he stayed or went. But I wished with all my heart he would stay.

'Stay, stay, stay', I thought. 'For just another hour, tonight.... always.'

'I'll stay', he said, 'but only if she asks me to', as he nodded my way. I smirked an 'Ok' secretly relieved. I mocked him, 'Please Peter stay?'

'Of course,' he said and walked over to me.

The others sauntered ahead of us, and without saying a word, he grabbed my hand. The summer sky roared, purple, orange and pink. The wooden bridge creaked with delight as our silent souls danced for joy across it. Something was happening; I didn't know exactly what it was. I was happy, elated, home.

Motown was gently rocking the old Dutch bar, with the 1960's jukebox. Worn carpets on tables and floor smothered in low orange light. The bartender served cold meat, cheese, and   bitterballen with a face like mustard.

Our gang of bandits took over the bar, singing, roaring, and laughing. Peter sat opposite me on the circular table; I could hardly breathe. The shape of his head, his Roman nose, his beautiful eyes, his heavy brows, his soft tanned hands. It was 2.30 in the morning and we were stumbling out of the bar.

'Tell me he doesn't have a girlfriend', I ordered Elsa. Her reply scorched my heart.

'I'm sorry, Sheila, he has a girlfriend and a little boy.' My heart sank.

I crawled onto the mattress on the floor in the dark, spinning, room. I was drunk in alcohol and in love with a man who had a partner and a child. And wasn't it just my luck?

I lay awake all night. My chest aching, head hurting, guts churning. Things like this didn't happen to me. They didn't happen to anyone. Falling instantly in love happened in movies, songs, operas, and poems but not in real life and certainly not to me. I simply did not believe in that stuff.

The next morning, I was barely awake, when Elsa handed me the phone.

'Did you miss me?', it was Peter.

'No' I hung up with fright. 'I can't do this', I thought.

He called back, 'Did you just hang up on me?'

'Yes', I said. 'What do you want?'

'You', his response. 'What are you doing today?'

'Going to town to shop', I croaked, my mouth as dry as a desert sandal.

'Ok', he said, 'maybe I'll see you later?'

'Ok', I murmured. I had to be careful in front of Elsa; she wouldn't approve and rightly so.

I had breakfast and got ready to go to town to buy clothes. I couldn't concentrate, I couldn't think, I couldn't see. I decided I would walk to town. I needed to be outside on the street where I might see him, where he might be, where he might pass me; at least we were in the same city. Still delicate, I changed my mind when I saw a tram in the distance. As I stood at the tram stop, I saw a white van pulling in slowly opposite me. It stopped across the street. I don't know how I knew, but I knew it was him. I had no idea what he drove, and I couldn't see him, but I just knew it was him and he was coming to see me.

As if in slow motion, like in a movie, he jumped out of the van and walked across the road towards me.

'I thought you were working today', I could barely speak. 'I was', he said, 'but I had to come see you. I've checked every tram stop all the way to town.' As we talked, my tram came and went. We ignored it as if it wasn't there. We walked back across the road and got into his van.

'Sorry about the mess', he says, as he throws cartons of cigarettes and empty bottles of water over his shoulder. We didn't speak as we drove into town. We both knew we shouldn't see each other but we both desperately wanted to. We went shopping. I bought some clothes. I didn't care what we did, once we were together. All day, we sat in an Irish bar talking.

'Tell me everything about you, from the beginning', his voice sweet, low and divine. And so I did; we talked all day until it was dark.

'Come on I'll drop you back', as we ran across the busy street, trams, cars, bikes, flying past, he took my hand. 'I've wanted to do that all day', he said. There we were two people holding hands, running across the street in a capital city, like so many people all over the world. To anyone, we looked like an ordinary couple, laughing, together, and in love ...

He felt like home. I felt the happiest, safest, the most wonderful I'd felt in years. I felt alive, seen, heard. Not like a ghost of myself or a shadow of a human in a life, an existence with everything but nothing of worth. I wanted to cling to him, scream for him, tell him I'd never felt this way before. I wanted to beg him not to go, to hold him, to plead for him to stay; stay, stay, stay with me and don't ever go. But I didn't need to scream, beg, or plead; he knew how I felt. He felt exactly the same way.

Back at Elsa's flat we could barely speak or look at each other.

'You leave on Wednesday?', he says as he leans his back against the window. The large green tree behind his head flush in full summer bloom, dances in the yellow light as I stand at the door, tears in my eyes and a lump in my throat. How cruel of nature, I thought, to be so full of life, to be so very beautiful, when my heart was obliterated ...

'I have to go. I can't ... ', he mutters and rushes past me. He was leaving. He jumps down three stairs, then stops and turns around. He stands and looks back up at me, his hand over his mouth, his head nodding from side to side. His pale blue Fred Perried chest heaving up and down as tears fall from his eyes. We both knew in that moment what was to be. My heart was broken for him and for me, too. I wanted to hold him, cling to him, consume him, fill every thought in his head, own him, be with him, love him.

My soul decimated, my world in ruins, empty, hollow, worthless. What good was my world without him in it?

Maybe, once, twice in your life, if you're really lucky or unlucky, you meet someone and fall instantly, insanely in love. My flight back to Dublin was a late one.

Shadow-shaded walls, the blinds half down, I tiptoe up the cranky, dimly lit stairs. The early hours, dark and sombre like my mood. Carly's dainty feet tapping sparingly on her wooden floorboards.

'Is that you She?', she says softly, our mother sleeping downstairs. I open her door and crumble to the floor.

'What happened, what happened you?', her life's blood drained from her face.

'I…. huuh…met….huuh…Elsa's brother…huuh… and fell…. in…. love.' Grief sodden tears flooded my face. 'What am I going to do? What am I going to do?', I gulp.

'What's wrong with that, that's good Sheila, that's good. What's wrong with that?', she asks confused.

'He has a partner and a little boy', I wept. 'Oh', she says, 'Oooh.' Our childhood memories of devastation caused by an affair never far. I stare at my teardrops on the dark wooden floor that catch the moonlight glow. Still dressed she helps me onto my feet, onto my bed and under a quilt. The memory of Esther on the stairs that desolate night haunts me; was it to be the same for me …

A wretched sorrow engulfs my being that wasn't to leave me for three long years.

Biological anthropologists and scientists say, when someone falls in love, neurochemicals flood the brain. These neurochemicals, such as dopamine and oxytocin, produce feelings of pleasure, elation, intense emotions, sleeplessness, sexual and emotional cravings. Loss of appetite, almost addictive obsessive behaviour, as well as extreme mood swings, are all part of this glorious phenomenon. One's emotions can run the gauntlet from the depths of despair to frenzied delirium and mine did all of the above. Some people in love act in a semi-normal fashion. Not I. I became a neurotic, compulsive, hysterical, obsessive, psychotic, mostly drunk, lunatic.

Not long after our meeting I moved to Amsterdam. I thought that by being there, I would make him want to leave his family. It didn't, he didn't. I tortured myself. It was craziness, but I couldn't help it, or didn't want to. I just wanted to be with him and if that meant living in the same city, then so be it. I handled falling in love so very badly. He was, for me, a cosy home after a traumatic journey. The symphony on a Monday morning bus ride. A place to rest my weary soul. Even drink didn't fill my hallow legs, not to mention, my even more hallow heart. The truth is I had an emptiness that only he could fill. He was a rejection I liked to re-enact. A trauma I liked to repeat. A scab I liked to pick. I thought about Esther and her broken heart, how it defined, and shaped her life, erased her dreams, cut short her prospects.

'Don't waste your life on a man that doesn't want you!' I loved her and vowed never to let a broken heart do that to me.

Aside from my broken heart, I loved Amsterdam. Not one to be completely beaten by any situation, I was defiant and decided I would make the most of being in that beautiful city. I hosted a karaoke night in an Irish bar, recorded jazz standards in the Conservatorium Amsterdam; and got the lead in a show. I auditioned for a musical with an excellent theatre company, for a successful production of a musical comedy set in the nineteen thirties. I played an English aristocrat, a part that was high camp, big eyes and shocked expressions. The musical genius and elegance that is Cole Porter, enhanced each scene. Despite the weekly weigh-ins and the dictatorial director, I had a great time and made some great friends.

Late nights in bars and gay clubs. Wine in parks, dinner parties in houses and on boats. Drunk dialling from a private number, buckled drunk cycling home at four in the morning. I was not destroyed, but I was a mess. I plotted, schemed, contrived, manipulated, lied, and engaged in every kind of ruse and manoeuvre to be with this man. Given a chance, every deed of skulduggery, would have, at least, been attempted. It was not to be. He was too good, too nice to cheat, unlike me. I would have sold my grandmother to be with him (but she was too precious!).

Too loyal to commit the final act. His betrayal was purely emotional and much deadlier for me. His reckless, unguarded heart crucified mine. In time, his communications became less frequent. I thought maybe he had gotten over it. It was my burden alone to carry. I saw him months later at a summer barbeque but my whole body was shaking so badly that I couldn't physically stand up and had to sit on the grass. I literally could not walk. I could see him, but he didn't come to me. His whole family was there and watching.

He left the party, having only just arrived. His sister told me later that he couldn't bear it. He said I wouldn't speak to him or even look at him. What could I do? What did it matter? There was nothing to be done anyway.

I learned about a year later that he had moved out of his home for six weeks after meeting me and slept on his sister's kitchen floor. His heart was broken too. Before pursuing me, he wanted to see if he could leave his life but, most importantly how it would affect his son. Though this news made me cry a little more. I was happy, happy I didn't imagine it. Happy, he did love me. Happy, I wasn't mad (but was). Happy he really was as good as I thought he was. He went back home to his life to his son, and I admired him for that. I must admit a smile escaped my lips when Elsa told me he'd gotten an Irish red setter dog on his return.

'She has the same colour hair as you', she says with a smile.

The Apple of Me Eye

The rain thrashed the window of my new apartment on the Sarphati Park, Amsterdam.

Empty and dark but for a mattress on the floor and a table accompanied by two vintage chairs, recycled, sturdy but battered like me. Beautiful paintings adorned the walls, originals on loan from Katherine. It was two years since I'd seen Peter, my affair with Amsterdam lasting much longer than the one I wanted with him. The phone rang as I tidied the place and attempted to clean the carpet with a dustpan and brush. I was expecting visitors. My friend, the beautiful Bulgarian concert pianist, was visiting me with her lovely son. He, at five years old, had shamed me into doing what my mother and all of my friends put together couldn't do, clean. When on a previous visit, he pointed at my carpet and said in Dutch 'Vies momma, vies!', which means dirty. He then instructed me in perfect French how to clean my house whilst lecturing me on the perils of germs and insects. He spoke four languages. I barely spoke English.

Tripping over the pile of dirty clothes on the floor and swearing at the bastard who had the temerity to ring the phone, I answered it.

'Hello!', my raised voice.

'Sheila, I'm going up to see Esther.' It's Carly. 'She's not well. There's something wrong with her. They don't know what it is yet, but she's in hospital. I'm going up to see her now. I have to go before the traffic gets bad', she rattles it out quickly.

'Oh ok', I say in shock. 'Will you tell her I was asking for her. I'll try to call her later. Tell her to keep her phone on. Tell her I lov.' Click. Carly hangs up.

As I clump around the solemn room, with the balcony doors open, I watch the rain fall in slanted sheets on the lush, parched trees. Images of Esther flash before me like a montage in my mind. A lemon and white tiny dress from Spain when I was three. The Spanish flamenco doll on the top shelf, 'You can hold it, but you can't play with her.' Dancing, cleaning, singing, parties. Nights in my twenties when I stayed with her after a night out. The time I nearly killed us in my blue Bambino ... The laughs of me when she jumped out of the car and ran down the road away from me, saying I was trying to kill her. The time we went shopping in Belfast, when the armed soldiers marched around the streets after us, and she jumped on the train without me. I lost the plot and screamed the platform down, accusing her of trying to desert me. She cried laughing all the way home, and for weeks after. 'The names she called me, Betty were inhuman', she tells my mother.

Her face, when as a teenager I reject her, and no longer want to stay with her and Nanny.

'There you are, stranger, I never see you anymore', says Esther, still resigned, sitting in her chair. The lonely hours, days, weeks, and years stretched behind and before her.

'I haven't seen you for months. There was a time when I couldn't move for you. Now, I never see you.'

Her desperation so thick in the air, it chokes me. I want to get away as fast as I can, and I did. When she was there, in front of me, I couldn't see her. I didn't want or need her. But now, oh now, I'd give anything to hold her, hug her, talk to her, and love her, like she did me.

Guilt sits on my chest; its burden blurs my teary soul's vision. How compassionate I am, in retrospect, I think to myself.

Back in her world, her little dog Bonnie jumps on her lap. Bonnie, named after *Scarlett O'Hara's* only child, this gruesome targer takes up most of her time. As do trips to the supermarket, caring for her sister's two young children and jaunts to my mother's house and to town on the bus.

A hard knock on my mother's front door, and I see her through the floral cloud of distorted glass.

'Where were you? You mad woman, there's a storm warning tonight.' I tell her, 'It's lashing out, you're soaked to the bone. Come on.'

'I don't care, I had to get out of that house, the four walls were getting in on me.' she pants.

'Give me that', I want to wheel her shopping trolley for her, but she tells me no.

'I need it to lean on. I can hardly breathe. Give me me mask please', she points and flops onto the chair in my mother's bedroom. I hand her the mask attached to an oxygen tank in her trolley; she gasps its air. My mother is in bed again, sick again, after years of bed-confining illness. We still don't know why... I give Esther her mask and a towel to dry her dripping hair. I make them tea and sandwiches, give her a warm cardigan and turn up the heating.

'Sheila', my mother calls down the stairs to the kitchen, 'Will you make me and Esther another hot cup of tea, and will you go to the chipper for fish'n chips for us?'

Illuminated in the orange glow from the two-barred electric fire, Esther sits on a chair at the side of my mother's bed. The floral curtains, bedspread and painted wallpaper decorate the cosy scene, while I pour the tea from my mother's favourite *Van Gogh* teapot. Two heated plates and a stack of batch bread and butter sit perched on the little coffee table, waiting for me to open the crispy brown paper bag with the steaming salt and vinegar scent. As they enjoy their fattening and seldom feast, I sip my tea, look at the television and earwig their conversation.

'I saw that *No Tears* series on contaminated blood on the television last night', Esther says to my mother. 'You had Nathaniel in 1977 wasn't that the year they were giving the poor women having babies the contaminated blood and you got the Anti-D giving birth, didn't you?' My mother's eyes dilate, flicker, her life's suffering racing through her brain. In that awful moment she told me later, she knew, in her heart of hearts, it was true.

'Oh God, don't say that, that's so frightening, most of those poor women are dead.'

'I don't mean to frighten you Betty, but it makes sense, the way. You've been so sick for so long, all of the symptoms are the same.'

'Uneducated', Esther was smart as a whip; she didn't miss a trick. She single-handedly diagnosed my mother's illness after years of doctors and consultants drawing a blank.

'Stop Esther! Stop! I'll call the doctor and ask him tomorrow. I just can't think about that now, that is just horrifying!', my mother raises her voice.

'Sorry Betty, I didn't mean to upset you', Esther quickly says. An uncomfortable silence envelops the room.

'It's ok, I know you're only trying to help me', my mother's smile comforts her. Moments pass as the two friends sit in a silent trance, the wind and galloping rain beat the window, with bullets of incessant hailstone pellets.

'Look at that rain Esther, have you ever seen anything like it?', my mother pensively asks.

'No Betty, never. It's biblical, biblical ... ' Esther slowly responds. The two friends, who have seen so much of life's happiness and heartache, sit together late into the wild and stormy evening. About to leave, I put my head around my mother's bedroom door;

'Night, I'm going out.' They can hardly hear me over the blaring music and shrieks of laughter. I see a sight that would warm the cockles of any heart. There they are, two of life's troupers, up dancing and laughing, like two teenagers to one of Esther's favourite songs, *That Yellow Dress* by Joe Brown. It's on my mother's favourite album, the brilliant *Dreamboats and Petticoats*.

Like Lazarus of old, two of life's injured parties are still defiant, resilient, hopeful. That beautiful moment in time will forever be etched in my mind, and in my heart.

The shock diagnosis later verified, after a lifetime of illness, shook my mother to the core. Years lost to a constant struggle while raising her children alone under the monumental strain of an unidentified albatross. A horrendous illness given to an innocent woman, took its toll on her life and ours. An illness that at times crippled her physically, psychologically, and socially. An unknown that couldn't be uncovered or explained, shattered her health and confidence for years.

The minimal, monetary compensation my mother received was an insult and could never replace the years of suffering she endured. But she wanted her day in court and got it. She wanted to tell her story and have it recorded, and she did like the valiant, articulate, brave warrior she was.

In the summer of 2005, she stood tall and told the Hepatitis C Tribunal that she was 'angry.' That in her adult life, having given birth to her fourth child, she received the Anti-D injection from a contaminated blood batch and that she would never again know the same level of exuberance or good health. She told the Tribunal that this was unforgivable. She spoke about how she was told by a consultant that she was 'one of the lucky ones.'

'Am I supposed to be grateful, I am one of the supposed "lucky ones" she asked the four judges sitting on the bench for the Tribunal. 'As opposed to what?', she continued. 'The poor women, mothers, wives, and grandmothers that are actually dead?'

She was concise, precise, brilliant, cutting, powerful, defiant.

From that day on, I saw the spiritual rebirth of my mother before my eyes. Her body though compromised, is stronger. Her spirit, reborn, soars and conquers. She travels the world, paints, has exhibitions, writes and illustrates the most beautiful children's books. She lives.

* * *

'Esther, can you hear me? It's me, Sheila', I say a day after Carly's phone call. 'I'm calling you from Amsterdam. Are you ok?'

'I'm ok. I'm ok, I can hear you. When are you coming home? They're letting me out the day after tomorrow', she gasps in a raspy, weak voice I've never heard before.

'I'll be home in a few days', I tell her. 'Don't worry. You'll be alright. I love you. I'll see you soon.' I can't hold back my tears, but I do swallow the lump in my throat and let them fall silently. I'm glad she can't see me now.

'Alright, when are you coming home?', she asks me again, her voice fading.

'In a few days', I tell her again. She whispers, 'Ok' and hangs up. A deep sadness pierces my soul. My one and only Esther is ill. I book my flight for the following Monday and pray she'll be ok.

It was almost an empty flight from Amsterdam. It landed at 12 noon.

'Esther called me every night for the past few months. Sheila she was afraid', my mother tells me, my suitcase still in the middle of the floor in our basement. The windows and French doors are open. The scent from my mother's sweet flowers in the front and back garden waft through our house. Sweet pea, lilac, yellow, pink, and white roses, freesia, pansies, lavender, apple, pear and plum trees, are just some of the beautiful flowers and trees she grows. She looks great today and is painting a stunning picture in the back conservatory accompanied by Erasure and our gorgeous fox terrier dog, Sam. He, too, suffers from

Stockholm syndrome and sits adoringly, enamoured and staring by her side. He, too, has had a tumultuous relationship with her. Some days, he is petted, stroked, coddled, and loved. On others, he is banished, shouted at, locked out and the recipient of a tirade of verbal abuse. Not only is the little fox terrier, sandy gold, and beautiful with the most enchanting brown eyes you ever saw, he is a wonderful magician and can make her breakfast, supper, or dinner disappear in one-eighth of a millisecond on any given day. On these occasions, he goes by the name of 'Ye little bastard', 'Ye f***ing bastard', or 'Ye poxbottle of a dog!' Depending on the offence.

My mother continues to tell me of Esther's late-night calls.

'She'd call me, and I'd sit and talk to her for hours in the middle of the night. Kiley stays with her most nights, the last year. She's wonderful to her.' The deep shame and regret I feel for not being there for Esther is unbearable. For being away, for neglecting her. But worse is the thought that she might not be in this world, that she is going to leave here without me. I can't bear it. I block out the seriousness of the situation of her illness. I don't go up to see her when I get home. I go out for a week and get drunk instead. Esther is in my auntie Vera's now. Vera is taking care of her. I still believe Esther has much longer than she has.

Early Monday morning my mother accosts me as I eat my breakfast.

'Sheila! When are you going to see Esther? You need to go up and see her. You can't leave it any longer. She doesn't have long', my mother's tone drops a boulder on my head. She is deeply concerned. I walk up the stairs in a trance and feel like I've just heard the news for the first time. I haven't, I've blocked it out. I don't want to admit that this could be it. I don't want to say goodbye. I don't want to see her because then I will have to acknowledge she was leaving. Leaving me. Leaving … me. I go upstairs, lay on my bed and cry my heart out for hours. A silent, maddening tape is on a loop and almost drives me to despair; don't leave me here, Esther. Don't leave me, don't leave me here without you, please. I beg her. From the pit of my stomach, I feel ill, numb, empty and so terribly sad. I decide then that I will see her the next afternoon.

The following day, Tuesday. 'I don't like Tuesdays. I never go anywhere on a Tuesday', my mother's voice ringing in my ears as I drive my sky blue *Mini Micra* up the road. The distance between us much shorter now that I am grown. The old Dublin streets of my childhood still look the same, though are a lot busier. Patrick Kavanagh is still sitting on the Grand Canal, waiting for the pub to open while he writes his beauties. The characters of Joyce's *Dubliners*, are still alive, bustling and well. Well, most of them anyway.

My heart is thumping as I knock on the door of the pebble-dashed house. It's not Esther's house, 'Me Nanny's', it's Vera's house up the road. My aunty opens the door.

'Come on in love, she's just in here.' I see a screen and look behind it. Esther is lying down in a bed in the front room with the blinds pulled down. Her body, tiny, frail, and cream. There was hardly any difference between her skin and the snow-white flannel net sheets. I sit on the chair beside her, fighting back tears. I quietly whisper, 'It's me, Sheila, I'll just sit here, you sleep.' With that, she opens her eyes wide, pushes herself up on her pillows, takes a second and puts out her hands like she's seeing a ghost.

Our eyes slowly stare and reflect our memories together. In each other's happiness and pain, a mirror of days long ago. Sunny days of pink plastic picnics in my Nanny's front garden; of Max Factor lipstick, dresses, and dolls; of Easter eggs and scorched country holidays; of Christmases with cosy pyjamas, hot water bottles, fur hats and mufflers; of Nanny's Sunday roasts and cups of hot tea. This silent, wordless exchange binds us in contentment, ease and knowing ... knowing that in all the world, our love is sacred, pure, free, limitless...

We know with sodden eyes and cheeks that words are unnecessary, pointless ...

Our hands intertwine but our souls, our souls are blended, welded, fused together from the beginning. In my mind, beyond the yellow sun and the starry blue sky, we run and sing and dance into the light. A galloping, dreaming adventure we once shared and will again. We hear the loud, warm but annoying voices of the people who were closest, but never knew. Never knew that roses smelled of magic perfume, that plastic tea sets held mystical cordials. That everyone else was plain and dull and that she, SHE was the most beautiful of them all!

'Clunk', the plate of well-meaning sandwiches by the clumsy cousin is lumped on the table.

Esther throws her eyes up to heaven ... 'What she think

we are, gorillas?', she croaks, barely audible ... we both laugh. 'Ah but she means well', she softly follows.

'I was waiting on you', she tells me.

'I know,' I say.

I want to tell her I couldn't see her because I couldn't let her go. How, why would I say goodbye to the one person in my life who truly could never see a fault in me? That loved me in spite of myself, my neglect, my selfishness, my lack of care for her. One of the few people in the world that I, with all my heart, had unconditionally loved. She was the freshest mountain spring that bathed and nourished my small body. She was my pal. We sit together and chat a little, but mostly, we sit in silence, both of us just glad we are together again.

I ask her if she needs anything. She tells me no.

'I love you', I tell her, trying to hold back more tears.

'I love you too', she tells me. Neither of us wants to let go.

'What are you crying for?', my aunt interrupts and asks her.

'Nothing', she mumbles. They didn't get it, but we did. It made me angry that at this time she was even asked such a question, but I have to let it go. I wish things were different. I wish I had my own place to take her to. I wish I could shelter her from prying eyes and visitors that came too late by years. But who was I to want to rescue her at this late stage myself?

On the way from my aunt's house I pass my Nanny's, now Esther's house. The acute sorrow I feel is so heavy in my heart I can barely take a breath. The memories of the home I stayed in, in my early childhood, packed with children with laughter, with stories. A home so busy you could hardly think or get a place to sit.

My grandmother already gone ten years; had a funeral fit for the queen that she was. A six horse-drawn carriage with plumes, her lifelong wish. She grew up with horses and carriages.

'My people were horse trainers', she told me. 'Me mother, father and uncles owned stables and property in Patrick Street. They had the contracts for Guinness's Brewery and had shares in *Guinness* and *Jameson*. The lot to be mine, before the solicitor sold the shares, the land, took the money and ran off to Australia.'

Today I can't eat when I get home or talk to my mother or anyone for that matter. I go straight to bed. The day after that, I go back up to see Esther again. Today she is lying on the bed and much weaker. She tells me to sit closer so she can tell me something.

'Are they still sitting there on the couch?', she whispers. 'What is she doing here? She nods at a relation's wife, incredulous that after years of hardly seeing them, they are now holding a vigil by her bed. I tell her to 'Shush don't mind them. Don't think about them, think about getting better.'

She looks at me and says nothing. Her once sparkling blue eyes faded.

Too broken to argue, I rub her cheek. The following day, she is unconscious. A beautiful angel in the form of a palliative care nurse keeps her comfortable. In the background, her sisters, brothers, nieces and nephews, the people who loved her, her whole life, sit around. They cry, whisper, sing, pray and laugh. I can't. I just want to be with her. The nurse tells me she may still be able to hear so I talk to her. I hold her hand and tell her, 'I'm here with you, I love you, get a rest, go to sleep.'

I sit with her as her chest rises one last time; she breathes her last breath and goes back home. Home to my Nanny, and to my Grandad. My Grandad, who for years, when Esther was in hospital as a child, took the bus if he had the money, or if he hadn't, hitched a lift on a pony and trap, or walked miles, to care for her for hours every evening.

Her body, immaculate, peaceful, loved, is finally at ease.

A body, that at six years old was injured while swinging on a rope from a lamppost. Years in braces, and countless operations, failed to prevent the excessive curvature of her spine on one side, that eventually pierced one of her lungs.

She was a trouper in a body that people stared at, that made life harder. I'd known her since I was a baby and she'd always been beautiful to me. She was beautiful. At fourteen, it dawned on me that people thought because she had a curve on her spine that she was 'disabled' ... She wasn't, she was very able and different, and smart, and funny, and witty, and gorgeous. And I laughed harder and talked louder than I needed to when I was with her, because she was amazing and I loved her ...

Now exempt, emancipated, free... from the limitations of the physical world. A world that confines, binds, boxes, and labels anyone who is a little bit unusual, that little bit more interesting. What is the body, only a vessel in this world, for a spirit, a soul? A soul like hers; wonderful, boundless, kind and loving, her playful spirit, as delightful, feisty and vivacious as a sparring kitten ...

In the days that follow we wake her. Family, friends, relations, neighbours come and go. Tea, cakes, sandwiches, stews and coddles are delivered to the door in huge quantities by neighbours and friends, decent people, Dubliners. Gifted so the family can just be; and immerse themselves in their grief. The room is silent as the priest anoints her body and blesses her, one last time for her journey home. The many candles that light the recesses of the darkened space, wave and flicker as silhouettes of bodies bent in prayer, sniffle, gulp and shuffle, one by one, to her coffin side. There, they touch her, mumble or cry in silence.

Esther is laid out in a beautiful open coffin. Her white hands, praying placed gently on her white cotton-covered chest, hold pale blue rosary beads. Her face lineless, smooth, tranquil, her eyes closed. 'She looks asleep', I whisper to my cousin Sarah. Her hair is brushed but not dyed; I wish she'd had her roots done, and I'd have put more make-up on her, I think to myself. But that was me; I always overdid it.

'You have me like a quare one; take it off!', she'd laugh when I did her makeup.

We pray decades of the Rosary and sit in candle-lit silence as the priest says the final prayers. We sing, tell stories about her, laugh and cry. But we don't leave her alone for the next two days lest she gets lonely on her journey to the other side.

'You were the apple of her eye. She adored you,

couldn't see a fault in you', my aunty Anne tells me. 'The charm bracelet is for you, it was always yours, she told us.'

'That's right, that's right, my auntie Bridie says.' Others nod in agreement.

'The charm bracelet. I forgot about that', I smile, the memory of me holding it up to the light. 'Can I have your charm bracelet when you die?'

Esther laughing, 'May God forgive you!'

I could say it didn't mean anything now, now that she was gone, but that would be a lie; it meant more, more to me, more than ever. I collected it sometime later from my reluctant aunt, but I made sure and got it. It was, after all, always mine.

'Can I borrow Esther's charm bracelet to wear on my twenty-first birthday?', my sweet cousin, the caller asks.

'No, I'm sorry, I've only just gotten it and I can't bear to part with it' I say

It reminded me of our precious times together, Esther and I. So precious, the connection with the beautiful bracelet so strong, as a little girl I tried it on nearly every day. I had it now and was never letting it go, not for even one day. Like the dolls on the stairs, Esther gave it to me, and it was mine!

Esther's soul lives on in me. When I didn't have the strength to go on, when my own spirit and body were about to give up. When I cried salty tears of suffering. When I had nothing left to give. I called on her, I prayed to her. Then like an in-built spiritual lightsabre that comes from being truly loved, an inner power rose in me; she answered my prayers, as did my Nanny, and in my hour of need they saved me.

His Last Adventure

'Don't speak for at least half an hour', my mother orders my grandfather. 'I just got the kids out the door', she says on her hands and knees, lighting the fire.

'Not a word out of me or me pal will you hear', he puts his finger to his mouth and smiles, rubbing the dog's furry head.

'I said not a word; I need a moment to get my brain together.' She gets up and heads to the sink, slowly washing her hands, she then dries them leaning on the counter with both elbows. She then lets out a sigh, wipes her forehead, puts the kettle on and turns back to the old man.

'Now Daddy, do you want tea, cake, and a small one? Yes, no, or all three?'

'All three', he laughs, 'if you don't mind.'

She cuts him a large slab of currant cake, stirs the sugar into his tea and pours him a whiskey. She pulls the small coffee table over to his side and places them one by one; 'Now Da, are you warm enough?'

'Oh yes', he says; 'Sure amin I in the lap a luxury? That's lovely, thank you.'

She sits beside him on the couch, eating her cold toast. I never remember her having a warm meal, she was always the last to eat, and so her food was always cold.

'That's a beautiful fire', he tells her.

'You taught me how to light a fire, Daddy; I think I was about four', she says, looking into the fire.

'That sounds about right', he chuckles. He taught her how to light fires, cycle a bike, fix a puncture, float a boat, steam wood to bend and make a guitar, fix a fuse board, and to put tinfoil into Christmas lights to make them work. She was his youngest girl, and his pal. He was in his 80s now and didn't go out as much and stayed in bed that little bit longer every day, but every morning, he still managed to go next door to our house for his breakfast, a chat, and 'a heat at the fire.' Though he had his own fire too, and it blazed with anything that burned from morning till night, briquettes, coal, anthracite, logs, shoes, cardboard, wood, and furniture. He also had asbestos fingers. They were constantly in the fire and never burned.

'I miss your mother', he told my mother one morning. 'I'm lost without her.' My grandmother, Sheila, had passed some twenty five years previous. She was married late in life for those days, in her thirties. He was the best-looking man on the street, and she was an elegant, somewhat reserved, beautifully dressed woman, a tailor by trade. He was besotted with her his whole life and sometimes got jealous if she talked to the insurance man, Mr Ven, for too long. My mother told me her and my Nanny, would roar laughing at the preposterousness of his notions. My mother adored her too.

'Your Granda made a run at poor Mr Ven out there earlier; he waved his stick at him and told him to; 'Go long outa dat!', my mother tells me, laughing hysterically one July afternoon. Both men were in their 80s.

* * *

'Have you a light there?', my Granda asks Carly as he lies on the stretcher in the back of the ambulance, a cigarette hanging from the corner of his mouth.

'Just wait. I'll get you one, Granda', she tells him.

'Ah, me oul segotia', he says to her.

She runs to hand him a bright pink lighter and just before he strikes his thumb off the tiny wheel, the ambulance man swipes it out of his hand.

'Jesus, Mary and Joseph, they're trying to kill us! Are you trying to blow us up, Mr!', the ambulance man says, plump and scarlet faced.

'Sure, I was only going to have a quick pull', my grandfather tells him. With that, the man whips the cigarette from the corner of his mouth.

'Carly, Carly', Granda calls. 'Will you do me Lotto numbers, you never know; we might win, we'll split it, and I'll bring you to Nova Scotia. I always wanted to go to Nova Scotia, will you come with me?'

'Oh yeah Granda, of course I will. I'd love to go', she says. She's just like him and later that day, packs a case.

'Great so, that's the plan', he says, wholly content and hell-bent on his next adventure. With that my mother gets into the back of the ambulance.

She says his passing was beautiful, magical, peaceful ...

She felt his soul leave the room through the open window and for a second, she says, she caught a glimpse of the mystery and miracle of life ...

A Miracle

I'd prayed to them before, my Nanny and Esther, but now, now, I plead, bully, and harass them, at the end of my tether, I collapse on the church floor, helpless, hopeless, nothing left to give.

'Help me Nanny, Esther, help me, I can't do it anymore I just can't. Help me, help me, yous said yous would never leave me! Well, where are yis now, help me. Yous better help me, I'm telling yis I can't do this anymore ...'

The dialysis, the violent headaches, the projectile vomiting for hours, seven operations, the tiredness, bald patches, my hair falling out in clumps from steroids, I was bloated, my body and spirit were breaking under the emotional and physical strain.

As I leave the church something incredible happens. I put my foot down to step off the single granite step, but it does not touch the ground. From the tips of my toes right up through my body, something moves through me. I am weightless, for a fraction of a second, elevated, lifted, carried. The message quick, clear, swift, direct like a laser beam. My grandmother before me holds out her hands; 'I'll carry you through this, don't worry.'

The message, a balm on my bealing soul. I know in this moment, as sure as the stars hang in the sky, that I am going to get a kidney transplant within the week. I know there is a God, and I know that I am deeply loved.

'I'm gonna get my kidney transplant in the next week.'

I turn to my friend whose only goal that morning was to join me for a coffee.

'I'm not joking Nuala; me Nanny just told me. She moved through me; she was just there, she said she'd carry me through it. Do you believe me? I'm deadly serious. Just this second as I stepped off the step, she lifted me up. She held out her hands and lifted me, for a split second my feet didn't touch the ground. I swear to you as I'm standing here, I may be struck down dead, she told me ...'

'I believe you Sheila; I believe you. I know she did ...', Nuala wipes a tear from her cheek and grabs my hand.

The following Monday, I go to see my mother to tell her what happened but before I could open my mouth, she interrupts me; 'I think you're getting your kidney transplant very soon. I went to bed last night and turned off the radio before I went to sleep. But at 1 o'clock in the morning, the radio came on at full volume and woke me up; something, someone, told me you were getting a kidney and soon.' She then blesses herself.

*   *   *

The next thing I know at 2.30 in the morning, the following Tuesday night, I'm scrambling around our dimly lit flat, throwing clothes into a plastic bag. We were living together less than a year. Not the tidiest person in the world, I manage to find semi-clean pyjamas, clean underwear, a pair of leggings and a black top.

'Get to the hospital in the next hour', the caller said.

There are four of us in the taxi on the way to the hospital, the driver, my boyfriend, me, and my grandmother. She's to the left of me in her mink coat. Though she's been dead years, she's beside me. That mink coat, the same one given to me when she passed. I wore it on a skiing trip to Bulgaria when I met the old Jewish man who owned the travel company. I'd complained about the cold water in the three-star hotel we were in, when the cantankerous receptionist who looked like she'd wrestled six bottles of vodka the night before, pointed to him. He shook my hand; 'Mr Keselowski, What's the problem?', he said.

I explained what the problem was, and asked him what he was doing in Bulgaria, when his travel company was in Ireland? He said he was checking on some properties he owned.

'How long are you in Ireland?', I asked him.

'Since the fifties', he said.

'Are you Jewish?', I asked.

'Why did you say that?', he said. 'No one's ever asked me that?'

I told him about how my grandmother, and her mother, had helped the Jews that arrived in Dublin, before, and after the Holocaust. My great - grandmother, a wealthy businesswoman, had a shop, houses and stables on Patrick Street; her brothers had the contracts for Guinness's to bring and take the grain. I told him how they gave the Jewish people who'd arrived, goods on 'tick', 'the slate', to pay later. How those Jewish friends got on in business and in turn, looked after my grandmother. How they were her friends and dressed my father for his confirmation, when some children didn't have shoes, he had a suit, overcoat and leather boots. Her friends, the Erlichs, the

Rubinsteins, the Goldwaters, worked and lived in the area around Clanbrassil Street and Leonard's Corner.

'What's your grandmother's name?', he asks me.

'Lilly', I say. I also told him her maiden name.

'Beautiful, lovely, kind Lilly, her Silver Cross pram, the Kosher butchers, Clanbrassil Street and Leonard's Corner!', he said.

'This is her coat I'm wearing', I laugh.

'Get your bags!', he said. 'Come straight back down here; I'm taking you to another hotel.'

'We could end up buried in a ditch; you haven't a clue who he is; he could be a mass fuckin murderer for all you know!' My cousin whispers in the back of the taxi that is creeping through the black, snow buried roads in the beautiful Bulgarian countryside, 'It's not funny!'

At last, we see lights in the distance. The doorman in a top hat takes our cases through the stunning marble entrance. The five-star hotel equipped with a spa, pool, hair salon and beauty therapist will be our new accommodation.

'These are my guests; they are not to spend a penny, look after everything for them', he tells the receptionists. And they did. We join Mr Keselowski for dinner, and into the night, he shared his fascinating story with us of how he escaped the nazi round up, of how he was the only survivor of his town, a town which previously had a population of ten thousand Jews. He told us of how he ended up in Italy as a mascot for the army and how as a young boy he found himself abandoned with trucks and ammunition. How he sold them to the local mafia in the nearest town, the old lady he lodged with, and how he sat in his room with cases of lira. From there, he figured out that London was the place to be. And from there, he made his way to Dublin.

Back in the taxi, on the way to the hospital my boyfriend closes his hands over mine and turns to face me.

'I love you', he says, looking into my eyes. I try not to cry.

'Didn't I tell you they were always with me; Nanny and Esther. Didn't I tell you me Nanny said I'd get a kidney transplant soon?'

When we arrive at the hospital, we are directed to a wing that was all but for a couple of nurses and doctors, deserted. The corridors dark, silent, looming deep grey shadows, and cold, deep blue walls unnerve and frighten me. We were brought to an empty room, there, we sit on the bed holding hands, waiting. A nurse came and took my bloods. It was now four in the morning.

'We may have a match for you; we need to carry out some more tests.' Max just nods and stares at me. He is holding my hand, silent, white, anxious, stunned like a deer in headlights. Our fingers are woven together, holding our future dreams.

His big, blue eyes shine with the water that floats in them, his long black lashes curl under his dark, worried brows. We were together, and I was so grateful for him ... I knew that night he loved me. My mind wandered back to another night, just a few years earlier. A night where at four in the morning, I arrive at his house twisted drunk and lean on his bell until he answers.

'What do you want?', he asks me as he opens the door.

'I want to come in', I slur.

'No. Go home. I have work in the morning, and I'm really not in the mood for this.'

'I want to come in', I demand; 'Just let me in.'

'No!', he walks me outside, hails a cab, and piles me into it, then slams the door.

Unfazed, I go home, send him a slew of abusive messages and vow never to speak to him again as long as I live. That lasted until I saw him out again, and I pretend like nothing ever happened ...

And here he is beside me now, holding my hand. At twelve noon the next day, the doctor came in and told us I was getting a kidney transplant; they had a match. Max walked beside me as I was wheeled to the pre-transplant theatre's pre-anaesthetic suite. He let go of my hand, and the doors closed.

I lay there in the bright lemon room, terrified, ecstatic, but I wasn't to be alone for long. I blessed myself and began to say the Rosary for my donor and his/her family. I mixed it up, it had been so long since I said it. I thanked them for their kindness and cried for their loss. I was overcome by their generosity at such a horrendous time in their lives. At no time was I ever told the sex, age, or identity of my donor, but I knew it was a man.

As I lay there praying and crying, he appeared before me. I could see his face at the end of my bed; he was a heavy man, not overweight, but well-built. He had dark hair and lashes and a face full of stubble. He was in his mid-forties. I knew it was my donor. I asked him to protect me and stay with me and thanked him. I told him I was so sorry for him, for his family, that his death had to happen, and again told him how grateful I was for his kidney. I promised him I would honour his life, try to be the best person I could be (I often fail miserably), help people and do my best to give them hope, like he had done for me. I was aware that after the transplant, there was a possibility of rejection, but I dared not even entertain such a thought.

There, in the silence of that room, my life flashed before me. I asked myself had I enjoyed my life? Was I happy that if I died tonight, that I had made the most of it? My answer was a resounding, YES, yes, yes, yes, I had a fucking ball! I'd travelled the world, lived in New York, San Francisco, and Amsterdam. I'd acted, sang, drank, partied and laughed all around the world with the most exciting people. I'd enjoyed myself thoroughly!

But most importantly, I had been loved ...

*   *   *

I'd never gone to college, but I always wanted to. In 2015, three months before my kidney transplant, I started at Kings Inns, and commenced my law studies. I'd always wanted to do it, and since I couldn't do much else, I thought, why not? And besides, if I failed, at least, I'd have an excuse, I was sick! After months of complications post-transplant, and years of mental torture and exams, I was miraculously called to The Bar of Ireland in October 2018. It was one of the proudest moments of my life. My father and mother cried at the ceremony.

Sometimes when I run down Church Street to the Four Courts, full of myself in my tabs, wig and barrister's gown, I can see my grandmother before me, pushing her pram on that very street, her bandaged legs, scarf tied under her chin. The little girl with the red pigtails running beside her, yapping away, tormenting the old lady. A tear falls from my eye ...

Some days I yearn for their fried bread and sweet tea, just to hear a 'Don't mind them!' 'What ails you?' 'You're the apple of me eye.' Years have gone by since I drove by their house and cried into my chest. Days when I thought if I banged hard enough on the door to 509, they'd have to answer, but not now. For now, I know that Esther and my Nanny are woven into the fibres of my very soul, stitched deep and knotted into the tapestry that is me. Long gone but always here ...

My darling mother passed as the sun rose against a stunning sky in the summer of 2020. I miss them all so dearly, but in my heart, I console myself with the memory of Esther and my mother on that stormy, magical night, when I put my head around the door ... there they are, dancing, happy, free ...

THE END

Can I Have Your Charm Bracelet When You Die?